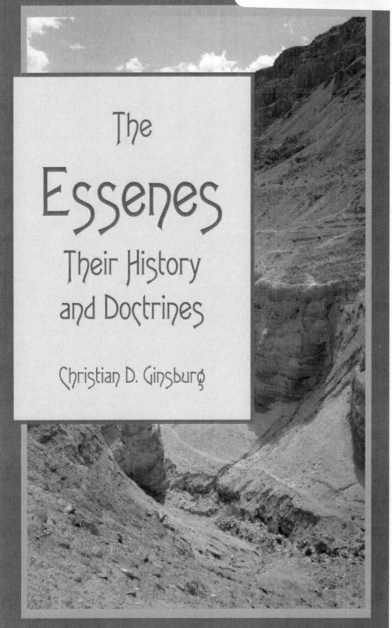

The
Essenes
Their History and Doctrines

Christian D. Ginsburg

The Essenes
Their History and Doctrines
Christian D. Ginsburg

A Cornerstone Book
Published by Cornerstone Book Publishers
An Imprint of Michael Poll Publishing
Copyright © 2018 by Cornerstone Book Publishers

Cornerstone Book Publishers
New Orleans, LA

Photograpic Reprint of the 1864 edition
First Cornerstone Edition - 2018

www.cornerstonepublishers.com

ISBN-13: 978-1-61342-305-9

MADE IN THE USA

THE ESSENES

THEIR HISTORY AND DOCTRINES.

AN ESSAY,

REPRINTED FROM THE TRANSACTIONS OF THE

LITERARY AND PHILOSOPHICAL SOCIETY OF LIVERPOOL.

BY

CHRISTIAN D. GINSBURG, LL.D.

ἐν παντὶ ἔθνει ὁ φοβούμενος αὐτὸν
καὶ ἐργαζόμενος δικαιοσύνην δεκτὸς αὐτῷ ἐστιν

ACTS X, 35.

CORNERSTONE BOOK PUBLISHERS
NEW ORLEANS, LOUISIANA
2018 PHOTOGRAPHIC REPRODUCTION

1864.

INDEX.

THE ESSENES.

I.

IT is very surprising that the Essenes, whose exemplary
virtues elicited the unbounded admiration of even the Greeks
and Romans, and whose doctrines and practices contributed
so materially to the spread of Christianity, should be so
little known among intelligent Christians. The current
information upon this remarkable sect or order of Judaism,
to be found in ecclesiastical histories and Cyclopædias, is
derived from the short notices of Philo, Pliny, Josephus,
Solinus, Porphyry, Eusebius, and Epiphanius. These seven
witnesses—of whom the first and third are Jewish philosophers, the second, fourth and fifth heathen writers, and the last
two Christian church historians—are all who, till within a very
recent period, have been subpœnaed before the tribunal of
public opinion, to give evidence as to the character of these
very much misunderstood and neglected Essenes.

Not only is this combined testimony insufficient, but it is
too much tainted with the peculiar dogmas of the respective
witnesses, to furnish the general reader with an unbiassed
notion of the character and doctrines of this ancient sect.
Philo and Josephus, writing in Greek and in apology for their
Jewish brethren, were too anxious to represent to the Greeks
and Romans every phase and sect of Judaism, as correspond-
ing to the different systems of Greek and Roman philosophy ;
Pliny, Solinus, and Porphyry, again, betray too great an
ignorance of the inward workings of the Jewish religion, and
too much prejudice against the Jews ; whilst Epiphanius draws
upon his imagination, and Eusebius simply copies the account
of Philo, with the well-known patristic pen. Nor can the

modern descriptions of the Essenes, as given in the histories of the church and in the popular Cyclopædias, be always relied upon when they profess to give the results of the afore-mentioned garbled scraps of ancient information ; since the writers are either too much afraid of, or too much pleased with, the marked resemblance between some of the doctrines and practices of Christianity and Essenism. Hence those who style themselves the true evangelical Christians are very anxious to destroy every appearance of affinity between Essenism and Christianity, lest it should be said that the one gave rise to the other; whilst those who are termed Rationalists multiply and magnify every feature of resemblance, in order to show that Christianity is nothing but a development of Essenism—so that the poor Essenes are crucified between the two.

The design of this essay is to give an impartial statement of the doctrines and practices of the Essenes ; to show their rise and progress, their relationship both to Judaism and Christianity, their numbers and localities, to trace the most probable signification of their name, &c., &c. To do this, I not only appeal to the seven stereotyped witnesses, but to the information upon this subject scattered throughout the Midrashim and the Talmud. But not to incur the charge of partiality, as well as to enable you to test my conclusions, I have collected all that the ancients have written upon this subject, and append to this paper the whole account which Philo, Pliny, Josephus, Solinus, Porphyry, Eusebius, and Epiphanius give of the Essenes.

The cardinal doctrines and practices of this sect are as follows :—They regarded the inspired Law of God with the utmost veneration. In fact, their adhesion to it was such that they were led thereby to pay the greatest homage to Moses, the lawgiver, and to visit with capital punishment any me of the brotherhood who blasphemed his name. The

highest aim of their life was to become the temples of the
Holy Ghost, when they could prophesy, perform miraculous
cures, and, like Elias, be the forerunners of the Messiah.
This they regarded as the last stage of perfection, which
could only be reached by gradual growth in holiness, brought
about through strictly observing the commandments and the
Levitical laws of purity contained in the Pentateuch, mortifying the flesh and the lusts thereof, and being meek and
lowly in spirit, inasmuch as this would bring them into closer
communion with him who is the Holy One of Israel. This
earnest desire to avoid everything which involved profanity in
the slightest degree and which might interpose between them
and the Deity, made them abstain from using oaths, because
they regarded the invocation, in swearing, of heaven or the
heavenly throne, or anything which represents God's glory,
as a desecration. Their communication was yea, yea; nay,
nay; whatsoever was more than these came of evil.

Their increased strictness in enforcing the observance of
the rigid Mosaic laws of Levitical purity, which were afterwards amplified and rendered still more rigid by traditional
explanations,[1] ultimately compelled the Essenes to withdraw

1 According to tradition there were four degrees of purity. 1. The ordinary
purity required of every worshipper in the temple (טהרת חולין). 2. The
higher degree of purity necessary for eating of the heave-offering (טהרת תרומה).
3. The still higher degree requisite for partaking of the sacrifices (טהרת הקודש).
And 4. The degree of purity required of those who sprinkle the water absolving
from sin (טהרת חטאת). Each degree of purity required a greater separation
from the impurities described in Leviticus xi, 24—xv, 28. These impure subjects were termed *the fathers of impurity*; that which was touched by them was
designated *the first generation of impurity*; what was touched by this again, was
called *the second generation of impurity*; and so on. Now, heave-offerings—the
second degree of holiness—became impure when touched by *the third generation*;
the flesh of sacrifices—the third degree of holiness—when coming in contact
with the fourth generation; and so on. These degrees of purity had even to
be separated from each other; because the lower degree was, in respect to the higher
one, regarded as impure, and any one who lived according to a higher degree of
purity became impure by touching one who lived according to a lower degree,
and could only regain his purity by lustrations (טובילה). The first degree
was obligatory upon every one, the other grades were voluntary. Before partaking of the heave-offering, the washing of hands was required; and before
eating of the flesh of sacrifices, immersion of the whole body was required
—Comp. *Babylonian Talmud, Tract Chagiga*, 18 b.

themselves altogether from the society of their Jewish brethren, to form a separate community, and to live apart from the world, since contact with any one who did not practice these laws, or with anything belonging to such an one, rendered them impure. This fear of coming in contact with that which is impure, as well as the desire not to be hindered in their spiritual communion with their Creator, also made the Essenes abstain from marriage; inasmuch as women, according to the law, are subject to perpetual pollutions in menstruum and child-birth (compare Lev. xii, 1—8; xv, 19—31), and as going to one's wife, even under ordinary circumstances, is regarded as defiling (*vide infra, p.* 39, *note* 19). There were, however, some weak brethren who could not be like the angels in heaven, neither marrying nor being given in marriage; these were allowed to take wives, but they could never advance to the highest orders of the brotherhood, and had, moreover, to observe laws specially enacted for married brethren and sisters.

Here, in their separation from the Jewish nation, whatever any one of them possessed was deposited in the general treasury, from which the wants of the whole community alike were supplied by stewards appointed by the whole brotherhood; so that they had all things in common. There were no distinctions amongst them, such as rich and poor, masters and servants; they called no one master upon earth, but all ministered to the wants of one another. They lived peaceably with all men, reprobated slavery and war, and would not even manufacture any martial instruments whatever, however great the temptation or the fear might be. They were governed by a president, who was elected by the whole body, and who also acted as the judge of the community. Trials were conducted by juries, composed, not as our juries are, of twelve persons, but of the majority of the community, or of at least a hundred members, who had to be unanimous in their verdict.

The brother who was found guilty of walking disorderly was excommunicated, yet was he not regarded as an enemy, but was admonished as a brother, and received back after due repentance.

As it was contrary to the laws of Levitical purity to buy anything from one who did not practice those laws, the Essenes had to raise the supplies of all their wants among themselves. In this they experienced no difficulty, as their food and raiment were most simple and very self-denying, and as each one of the community willingly took his share of work in the department in which he most excelled. Some were engaged in tilling the ground, some in tending flocks and rearing bees, some in preparing food, some in making the articles of dress, some in healing the sick, and some in instructing the young; whilst all of them devoted certain hours to studying the mysteries of nature and revelation and of the celestial hierarchy. They always got up before the sun rose, and never talked about any worldly matters till they had all assembled together and, with their faces turned towards the sun, offered up their national hymn of praise (המאיר לארץ) for the renewal of the light of the day. This done, every one betook himself to his work, according to the directions of the overseers, and remained at it till the fifth hour (or eleven o'clock, a.m.), when the labour of the forenoon regularly terminated. All of them again assembled together, had a baptism in cold water, put on their white garments, the symbol of purity, and then made their way to the refectory, which they entered with as much solemnity as if it were the temple. The meal was a common one; and each member took his seat according to the order of age. Those of the brethren who were the bakers and cooks then placed before each one a little loaf of bread and a dish of the most simple food, consisting chiefly of vegetables as they ate very little animal flesh, and the repast commenced after the priest had invoked God's blessing upon it. A mysterious silence was observed during the meal, which had the character of a sacrament, and may have been designed as a substitute for the sacrifices which they refused to offer in the temple. The priest concluded it by offering thanks to the Bountiful Supplier of all our wants, which was the signal of dismissal. Hereupon all withdrew, put off their white and sacred garments, and dressed themselves in their working clothes, resumed their several employments which they had to do according to the directions of the overseers till the evening, when they assembled again to partake of a common meal. But though every thing was done under the directions of the overseers, and the Essenes had even to receive their presents through the stewards, yet in two things they were at perfect liberty to act as they pleased, viz., they could relieve the distressed with as much money as they thought proper, and manifest their compassion for those who were not of the brotherhood as much as they liked, and whenever they liked. Such was their manner of life during the week days.

The Sabbath they observed with the utmost rigour, and regarded even the removal of a vessel as labour, and a desecration of this holy day. On this day they took special care not to be guilty of forsaking the assembling of themselves together, as the manner of some is. Ten persons constituted a complete and legal number for divine worship in the synagogue, and in the presence of such an assembly an Essene would never spit, nor would he at any time spit to his right hand. In the synagogue, as at meals, each one took his seat according to age, in becoming attire. They had no ordained ministers, whose exclusive right it was to conduct the service; any one that liked took up the Bible and read it, whilst another, who had much experience in spiritual matters, expounded what was read. The distinctive ordinances of the brotherhood, as well as the mysteries connected with the Tetragrammaton and the angelic worlds were the prominent topics of Sabbatic instruction. Every investigation into the causes of the phenomena both of mind and matter was strictly forbidden, because the study of logic and metaphysics was regarded as injurious to a devotional life.

Celibacy being the rule of Essenism, the ranks of the brotherhood had to be filled up by recruits from the Jewish community at large. They preferred taking children, whom they educated most carefully and taught the practices of the order, believing that of such the kingdom of heaven is best made up. Every grown-up candidate (ὁ ζηλῶν) had to pass through a noviciate of two stages, which extended over three years, before he could be finally admitted into the order. Upon entering the first stage, which lasted twelve months, the novice (νεοσύστατος) had to cast all his possessions into the common treasury. He then received a copy of the regulations of the brotherhood (δίαιταν τοῦ τάγματος), as well as a spade (σκαλίς ἀξινάριον=יָתֵד), to bury the excrement, (comp. Deut. xxiii, 12—14,) an apron (περίζωμα=אֵזוֹר), used at the lustrations, and a white robe (λευκὴν ἐσθῆτα=בֶּגֶד לָבָן) to put on at meals, being the symbols of purity. During the whole of this period he was an outsider, and was not admitted to the common meals, yet he had to observe some of the ascetic rules of the Society. If, at the close of this stage, the community found that he had properly acquitted himself during the probationary year, the novice was admitted into the second stage, which lasted two years, and was called an approacher (προσιὼν ἔγγιον). During the period which lasted two years he was admitted to a closer fellowship with the brotherhood, and shared in their lustral rites (καθαρωτέρων πρὸς τῶν ἀγνείαν ὑδάτων μεταλαμβάνει), but was still not admitted to the common meals (εἰς τὰς συμβιώσεις), nor to any office. If he passed satisfactorily through the second stage of probation, the approacher became an associate, or a full member of the society (ὁμιλητὴς,

ὅς εἰς τὸν ὅμιλον ἐγκρίνεται═חבר), when he was received into
the brotherhood and partook of the common meal (συμβιωτής).

Before, however, he was made *a homiletes*, or finally admitted into close fellowship, he had to bind himself by a
most solemn oath (this being the only occasion on which
the Essenes used an oath) to observe three things. 1. *Love to
God.* 2. *Merciful justice towards all men;* especially to honor
nobody as master, to avoid the wicked, to help the righteous,
to be faithful to every man, and especially to rulers (τοῖς
κρατοῦσιν), for without God no one comes to be ruler. And
3. *Purity of character*, which implied humility, love of truth,
hatred of falsehood, strict secresy towards outsiders, so as not
to divulge the secret doctrines (μυστήρια) to any one, and perfect openness with the members of the order, and, finally,
carefully to preserve the books belonging to their sect (τὰ τῆς
αἱρέσεως αὐτῶν βιβλία), and the names of the angels (τὰ τῶν
ἀγγέλων ὀνόματα) or the mysteries connected with the *Tetragrammaton* (שם המפורש) and the other names of God and
the angels, comprised in the theosophy (מעשה מרכבה) as well
as with the cosmogony (מעשה בראשית) which also played
so important a part among the Jewish mystics and the Kab-
balists.

The three sections consisting of candidate (ὁ ζηλῶν), approacher (πέροσιὼν ἕγγιον), and associate (ὁμιλητής, ὅς εἰς τὸν ὅμιλον
ἐγκρίνεται), were subdivided into four orders, distinguished from
each other by superior holiness. So marked and serious were
these distinctions, that if one belonging to a higher degree
of purity touched one who belonged to a lower order, *i.e.*,
if one of the fourth or highest order came in contact with one
of the third or lower order, or if one of the third touched one
of the second order, or if one of the second order touched
one of the first or lowest order, he immediately became impure, and could only regain his purity by lustrations. From
the beginning of the noviciate to the achievement of the

highest spiritual state, there were *eight* different stages which marked the gradual growth in holiness. Thus, after being accepted as a novice and obtaining *the apron* (זרין—περίζωμα) the symbol of purity, he attained (1) to the state of *outward* or *bodily* purity by baptisms (זריזות מביאה לידי נקיות). From this state of bodily purity he progressed (2) to that stage which imposed abstinence from connubial intercourse (נקיות מביאה לידי פרישות), or to that degree of holiness, which enabled him to practise celibacy. Having succeeded in mortifying the flesh in this respect, he advanced (3) to the stage of *inward* or *spiritual* purity (פרישות מביאה לידי טהרה). From this stage again he advanced (4) to that which required the banishing of all anger and malice, and the cultivation of a meek and lowly spirit (טהרה מביאה לידי ענוה). This led him (5) to the culminating point of holiness (ענוה מביאה לידי החסידות). Upon this summit of holiness he became (6) the temple of the Holy Spirit, and could prophesy (חסידות מביה לידי רה"ק). Thence again he advanced (7) to that stage in which he was enabled to perform miraculous cures, and raise the dead (רוח הקדש לידי תחה"מ). And finally, he attained (8) to the position of Elias the forerunner of the Messiah (תחה"מ לידי אליהו).

The earnestness and determination of these Essenes to advance to the highest state of holiness were seen in their self-denying and godly life; and it may fairly be questioned whether any religious system has ever produced such a community of saints. Their absolute confidence in God and resignation to the dealings of Providence; their uniformly holy and unselfish life; their unbounded love of virtue, and utter contempt for worldly fame, riches or pleasure; their industry, temperance, modesty and simplicity of life; their contentment of mind and cheerfulness of temper; their love of order, and abhorrence of even the semblance of falsehood; their benevolence and philanthropy; their love for the brethren, and their following peace with all men ; their hatred of slavery and war ; their tender regard for children, and reverence and anxious care for the aged ; their attendance on the sick, and readiness to relieve the distressed ; their humility and magnanimity ; their firmness of character and power to subdue their passions ; their heroic endurance under the most agonizing sufferings for righteousness' sake ; and their cheerfully looking forward to death, as releasing their immortal souls from the bonds of the body to be for ever in a state of bliss with their Creator—have hardly found a parallel in the history of mankind. No wonder that Jews, of different sects, Greeks and Romans, Christian church historians, and heathen writers have been alike constrained to lavish the most unqualified praise on this holy brotherhood. It seems that the Saviour of the world, who illustrated simplicity and innocence of character by the little child which he took up in his arms, also showed what is required for a holy life in the Sermon on the Mount by a description of the Essenes. So remarkably does this brotherhood exemplify the lessons which Christ propounds in Matth. chap v., &c.

This leads us to consider the question about the origin of this brotherhood, and their relationship to Judaism and Christianity. The assertion of Josephus that they "live the same kind of life which among the Greeks has been ordered by Pythagoras" (vide infra, p. 226, § 4,) has led some writers to believe that Essenism is the offspring of Pythagorism. The most able champion for this view is Zeller, the author of the celebrated *History of Philosophy*. He maintains[2] " that Essenism, at least as we know it from Philo and Josephus, has, in its essence, originated under Greek and especially under Pythagorean influences," and tries to support his conclusion by the following summary of the supposed resemblances between Neo-Pythagorism and Essenism. (1) " Both strive to attain to superior holiness by an ascetic life.

2 Geschichte der Philosophie, vol. iii, part ii, p. 583 ff.

(2) Both repudiate animal sacrifices, the eating of animal food, wine and marriage. (3) Both of them are, however, not quite agreed among themselves about the latter point ; for on both sides there are some who recommend marriage, but restrict connubial intercourse to procreation. (4) Moreover, both demand simplicity of life. (5) Both refrain from warm baths. (6) Both wear white garments, especially at dinner time. (7) Both lay the greatest value upon their purification and eschew everything unclean. (8) Both prohibit oaths, because a pious man does not require them. (9) Both find their social ideal in institutions which it is true were only realized by the Essenes, and in living together with perfect community of goods and unconditional subordination of individuals to their overseers. (10) Both insist on strict secresy about their schools. (11) Both like symbolic representations of their doctrines. (12) Both support themselves on an allegorical interpretation of ancient traditions, whose authority they recognise. (13) Both worship higher powers in the elements, and pray to the rising sun. (14) Both seek to keep everything unclean from their sight, and for this reason have peculiar prescriptions about the discharge of the duties of nature. (15) Both cultivate the belief in intermediate beings between the supreme Deity and the world. (16) Both devote themselves to magic arts. (17) Both regard above all things the gift of prophesy as the highest fruit of wisdom and piety, and both boast to possess this gift in their most distinguished members. (18) Finally, Both corroborate their peculiar mode of life with a dualistic view of the relation of the spirit and matter, good and evil. (19) Both agree especially in their notions about the origin of the soul, its relationship to the body, and about a future life, only the doctrine of transmigration of souls seems not to have been known among the Essenes."[3]

3 The figures before each point of comparison do not exist in the original German ; I have inserted them in the translation in order to facilitate the references to these different points of comparison.

Striking as these resemblances may appear, it will be seen on a closer examination that some of the points which constitute this comparison do not exist in Essenism, that others are either due to the coloring of Josephus or have their origin in Judaism, that the difference between Pythagorism and Essenism are far more numerous and vital than the parallels, and that Zeller's conclusion is therefore not warranted. I shall examine these points seriatim.

(1) Asceticism is not foreign to Judaism. We meet with individuals who voluntarily imposed upon themselves ascetic life to be able, as they thought, to give themselves more entirely to the service of God by mortifying the lusts of the flesh, at a very early period of Biblical history; and we need only to refer to the regulations about Nazarites (Numb. vi. 1-21), to the case of Manoah and his wife (Judg. xiii.), to the life of Elijah (1 Kings xviii.-xix.) to the practices of the Rechabites throughout the Scriptures, of persons abstaining from the good things of this world, to see how the Essenes, without (Jer. xxxv. 2, &c.), and to the numerous instances which occur copying the Pythagoreans or any other heathen fraternity, would naturally conclude that asceticism is conducive to a devotional life. (2) As to the repudiation of animal sacrifice, animal food, wine, &c., to which Zeller refers in the second point of comparison, I submit that the Essenes *did not repudiate* animal sacrifices, but that they *could not* offer them on account of the different view which they had about holiness, as Josephus most distinctly declares *(vide infra p. 52),* that neither Philo nor Josephus says a word about their objecting to eat animal flesh or drink wine, and that their celibacy arose from an extension of a law contained in the Pentateuch. Besides, it is not quite so certain that the Pythagoreans did not offer animal sacrifices; Diogenes Laertius and others positively state that Pythagoras himself sacrificed a hecatomb upon his discovering what is called the

Pythagoric theorem, *i.e.* that, in a right angled triangle, the
square of the hypothenuse is equal to the sum of the squares
of the sides.[4]   (4) The fourth comparison about simplicity
of life is involved in the first.   (5) The statement in the
fifth comparison, that the Essenes refrain from warm baths,
is purely imaginary ; (6, 7) whilst the white garments and the
purifications mentioned in the sixth and seventh parallels are
strictly Jewish and Biblical.   As symbolic of purity the priests
were required to clothe themselves in white linen (Exod.
xxviii. 39-42 ; Levit. vi. 10 ; xvi. 4), and the saints in heaven,
washed and cleansed from all impurity, are to be clad in white
garments (4 Esdras ii. 39-45 ; Enoch lxi. 18 ; Rev. iii. 4 ;
vi. 11 ; vii. 9, 14 ; xix. 8) ; soiled garments are regarded as
emblematic of impurity (Zech. iii. 3, &c.)   Inseparably connected therewith are the frequent purifications or washings
enjoined on the priests before entering into the presence of
God to perform religious acts (Levit. xvi. 4 ; 2 Chron. xxx.
19), and on the people generally after coming in contact with
anything impure (Levit. xi. 25, 40 ; xv. 5-24).   The white
garments and the frequent purifications of the Essenes, who
strove to live after the highest degree of Levitical purity,
were therefore in perfect harmony with exaggerated Judaism.
(8) As to the assertion in comparison 8 that the Pythagoreans prohibited oaths, it is well known that they did use
oaths on important occasions, and that they held it to be most
sacred to swear by the number four, which they represented
by ten dots in the form of a triangle, so that each side consisted
of four dots, as follows :—

$$\begin{matrix} & & \bullet & & \\ & \bullet & & \bullet & \\ \bullet & & \bullet & & \bullet \\ \bullet & & \bullet & & \bullet & \bullet \end{matrix}$$

4 Comp. Diog. Laert. de Vitis Philosophorum, lib. viii. Vit. Pythagor. xii.   It
s true that Cicero represents Cotta as giving no credit to this story, because, as

B

The community of goods, the secresy about their institutions, the symbolic representation of their doctrines, &c., mentioned in comparisons 9, 10, 11, 12, are the natural result of their manner of life. (13) That they worshipped the sun is not borne out by fact, (14) whilst their peculiar manner in performing the functions of nature is in accordance with the injunction of Scripture (Deut. xxiii. 13, 15), which the Essenes, as the spiritual host of the Lord, applied to themselves. (15) As to their very peculiar belief in intermediate beings between the Deity and the world, mentioned in the fifteenth point of comparison, I can only say that Philo and Josephus say nothing about it. (16) Their devotedness to the study of the magic arts was restricted to miraculous cures, and was not peculiar to them; since tradition had made Solomon the author of books on magical cures and exorcisms, and Josephus tells us (*vide infra, p.* 44, *note* 35) that he had seen other Jews performing these magic cures. (17) Neither is there anything foreign in the opinion, that the power to foretel future events can only be obtained by leading a life of preeminent holiness, for this was the common belief of the Jews, though it is true that the Essenes were the only section of the Jewish community who as a body strove to obtain the gift of prophecy. It, however, must not be forgotten that others too laid claim to this gift. Josephus tells us that when brought as prisoner of war before Vespasian, he addressed the Roman general as follows :—" Thou, Vespasian thinkest that thou hast simply a prisoner of war in me, but I appear before thee as a prophet of important future events. If I had not to deliver to thee a message from God, I would have known what the Jewish law demands, and how a general ought to die. Dost thou want to send me to Nero? For what? Will his successors, who ascend the throne before thee, reign

he apprehends, Pythagoras never offered animal sacrifices (*De Natura Deorum, lib.* iii. *cap.* xxxvi.), but it is also related by Athenæus (*Deipnosoph. lib.* x.), Plutarch and others.

long on it? No! thou, Vespasian, wilt be emperor and autocrat—thou, and this thy son." (*Jewish War*, iii. 8, § 9). This prophecy of ~~Josephus is~~ also recorded by the celebrated Roman historian Dion Cassius who ~~says~~: "Josephus, a Jew, was taken prisoner by him (i.e. Vespasian), and put in chains; but he smilingly addressed him: ' Thou puttest me now in chains, but thou wilt loose them again, after twelve months, as emperor'" (*lib.* lxvi. *c.* 1); and by Tacitus (*lib.* v. *c.* 13). What Zeller says in comparisons 18 and 19 about their dualistic view of the relationship of spirit and matter, good and evil, and their notions of the origin of the soul, is entirely owing to Josephus' colouring of the subject, as may be seen from the notes on the extracts from this historian in the second part of this Essay.

Having thus shown that the parallels between Pythagorism and Essenism are more imaginary than real, and that the few things which might be considered as being analagous are unimportant, and are such as will naturally develop themselves among any number of enlightened men who devote themselves almost exclusively to a contemplative religious life, I shall now point out some of the vital differences between the two brotherhoods. 1. The Pythagoreans were essentially polytheists; the Essenes were real monotheistic Jews, worshippers of the Holy One of Israel. 2. The Pythagoreans clustered round Pythagoras as the centre of their spiritual and intellectual life, and estimated the degree of perfection of any of the members by the degree of intimacy which he enjoyed with Pythagoras: the Essenes regarded the inspired Scriptures as their sole source of spiritual life, and called no man master on earth, every one having the same right to teach, and being alike eligible for all the offices in the commonwealth. 3. The Pythagoreans favored matrimony, and we are told that Pythagoras himself had a wife and children; whilst celibacy was the rule of

Essenism, marriage being the exception. 4. The Pythagoreans believed in the doctrine of metempsychosis, which led them to abstain from eating animal flesh, because human souls migrated into animals , and made Pythagoras once intercede in behalf of a dog that was being beaten, because he recognised in its cries the voice of a departed friend : the Essenes believed no such thing. 5. Scientific studies, such as mathematics, astronomy, music, &c., formed an essential part of the Pythagorean system : Essenism strictly forbade these studies as injurious to a devotional life. 6. Pythagorism was occupied with investigating the problems of the origin and constitution of the universe : Essenism regarded such inquiries as impious, and most implicitly looked upon God as the creator of all things. 7. Pythagorism taught that man can control his fortune and overrule his circumstances : Essenism maintained that fate governs all things, and that nothing can befal man contrary to its determination and will. 8. Pythagorism enjoined ointment to be used by its followers : the Essenes regarded it as defilement. 9. The Pythagoreans had a sovereign contempt for all those who did not belong to their ranks : the Essenes were most exemplary in their charity towards all men, and in their unbounded kindness to those who were not of the brotherhood. 10. The Pythagoreans were an aristocratical and exclusive club, and excited the jealousy and hatred not only of the democratical party in Crotona, but also of a considerable number of the opposite faction, so much so that it speedily led to their destruction : the Essenes were meek and lowly in spirit, and were so much beloved by those who belonged to different sects, that Pharisees and Sadducees, Greeks and Romans, Jews and Gentiles, joined in lavishing the highest praise upon them.[5]

5 An excellent account of the Pythagorean system is given by Zeller, Geschichte der Philosophie. Erster Theil, Tübingen, 1856, pp. 206–365 ; Grote, History of Greece. vol. iv. London, 1857, pp. 527–553 ; and Mason, in Smith's Dictionary of Greek and Roman Biography and Mythology, Article PYTHAGORAS.

As to the relationship which Essenism bears to Judaism,
the very fact that the Essenes, like the other Jews, professed
to be guided by the teachings of the Bible, and that a rupture
between them and the Jewish community at large is nowhere
mentioned, but that on the contrary they are always spoken
of in the highest terms of commendation, would of itself be
sufficient to prove it. In doctrine, as well as in practice, the
Essenes and the Pharisees were nearly alike. Both had four
classes of Levitical purity, which were so marked that one who
lived according to the higher degree of purity, became impure
by touching one who practised a lower degree, and could only
regain his purity by lustration. Both subjected every appli-
cant for membership to a noviciate of twelve months. Both
gave their novices an apron in the first year of their probation.
Both refused to propound the mysteries of the cosmogony
and cosmology to any one except to members of the society.
Both had stewards in every place where they resided to supply
the needy strangers of their order with articles of clothing
and food. Both regarded office as coming from God. Both
looked upon their meal as a sacrament. Both bathed before
sitting down to the meal. Both wore a symbolic garment on
the lower part of the body whilst bathing. Amongst both the
priest began and concluded the meal with prayer. Both
regarded ten persons as constituting a complete number for
divine worship, and held the assembly of such a number as
sacred. Amongst both of them none would spit to the right
hand in the presence of such an assembly. Both washed after
performing the functions of nature. Both would not remove a
vessel on the Sabbath. And both abstained from using oaths,
though it is true that the Essenes alone uniformly observed
it as a sacred principle. The differences between the Essenes
and the Pharisees are such as would naturally develope themselves in the course of time from the extreme rigour with
which the former sought to practise the Levitical laws of

purity. As contact with any one or with anything belonging to any one who did not live according to the same degree of purity, rendered them impure according to the strict application of their laws, the Essenes were in the first place obliged to withdraw from intercourse with their other Jewish brethren, and form themselves into a separate brotherhood. Accordingly the first difference between them and the others was that they formed an isolated order. The second point of difference was on marriage. The Pharisees regarded marriage as a most sacred institution, and laid it down as a rule that every man is to take a wife at the age of eighteen (Comp. Aboth v. 21), whilst the Essenes were celibates, which, as we have seen before, also arose from their anxiety to avoid defilement. Hence the declaration in Aboth d. R. Nathan—" *there are eight kinds of Pharisees ; . . . and those Pharisees who live in celibacy are Essenes*" (c. xxxvii.).[6] The third difference which existed between them and the Pharisees, and which was also owing to the rigorous application of the Levitical laws of purity, was that they did not frequent the temple and would not offer sacrifices. And fourthly, though they firmly believed in the immortality of the soul, yet, unlike the Pharisees, they did not believe in the resurrection of the body.

The identity of many of the precepts and practices of

6 R. Nathan, the Babylonian as he is called, was Vice-President of the College in Palestine, under the Presidency of Simon III. b. Gamaliel II. A.D. 140. The above-quoted work of which he is the reputed author, as indicated by its title, אבות דרבי נתן i.e. *the Aboth of R. Nathan*, is a compilation of the apothegms and moral sayings of the Jewish fathers (אבות), interspersed with traditional explanations of divers texts of Scripture, consisting of forty-one chapters. Both the historian and moral philosopher will find this work an important contribution to the literary and philosophical history of antiquity. It is printed in the different editions of the Talmud, and has also been published separately with various commentaries, in Venice, 1622 : Amsterdam, 1778, &c., &c.; and a Latin translation of it was published by our learned countryman, Francis Taylor, under the title of *R. Nathanis Tractatus de Patribus, latine cum Notis. London*, 1654, 4to. Comp. Zunz, Die gottesdienstlichen Vorträge der Juden. Berlin, 1832, p.p. 108, 109; Fürst, Kultur-und Literaturgeschichte der Juden in Asien. Leipzig, 1849, p. 16 ff; by the same author, Bibliotheca Judaica, volume iii. Leipzig, 1863, p. 19 ff; Steinschneider, Catalogus Libr. Hebr. in Bibliotheca Bodleiana col. 2,032 ff.

Essenism and Christianity is unquestionable. Essenism urged on its disciples to seek first the kingdom of God and his righteousness: so Christ (Matt. vi. 33; Luke xii. 31). The Essenes forbade the laying up of treasures upon earth so Christ (Matt. vi. 19-21). The Essenes demanded of those who wished to join them to sell all their possessions, and to divide it among the poor brethren: so Christ (Matt. xix. 21; Luke xii. 33). The Essenes had all things in common, and appointed one of the brethren as steward to manage the com mon bag; so the primitive Christians (Acts ii. 44, 45; iv. 32-34; John xii. 6; xiii. 29). Essenism put all its members on the same level, forbidding the exercise of authority of one over the other, and enjoining mutual service; so Christ (Matt. xx. 25-28; Mark ix. 35-37; x. 42-45). Essenism commanded its disciples to call no man master upon the earth; so Christ (Matt. xxiii. 8-10). Essenism laid the greatest stress on being meek and lowly in spirit; so Christ (Matt. v. 5; xi. 29). Christ commended the poor in spirit, those who hunger and thirst after righteousness, the merciful, the pure in heart, and the peacemakers; so the Essenes. Christ combined the healing of the body with that of the soul; so the Essenes. Like the Essenes, Christ declared that the power to cast out evil spirits, to perform miraculous cures, &c., should be possessed by his disciples as signs of their belief (Mark xvi. 17; comp. also Matt. x. 8; Luke ix. 1, 2; x. 9). Like the Essenes, Christ commanded his disciples not to swear at all, but to say yea, yea, and nay, nay. The manner in which Christ directed his disciples to go on their journey (Matt. x. 9, 10) is the same which the Essenes adopted when they started on a mission of mercy. The Essenes, though repudiating offensive war, yet took weapons with them when they went on a perilous journey; Christ enjoined his disciples to do the same thing (Luke xxii. 36). Christ commended that elevated spiritual life, which enables a man to abstain from marriage for the kingdom of heaven's sake, and which cannot be attained by all men save those to whom it is given (Matt. xix. 10–12 ; comp. also 1 Cor. viii.) ; so the Essenes who, as a body, in waiting for the kingdom of heaven (מלכות השמים) abstained from connubial intercourse. The Essenes did not offer animal sacrifices, but strove to present their bodies a living sacrifice, holy and acceptable unto God, which they regarded as a reasonable service ; the Apostle Paul exhorts the Romans to do the same. (Rom. xii. 1). It was the great aim of the Essenes to live such a life of purity and holiness as to be the temples of the Holy Spirit, and to be able to prophesy : the apostle Paul urges the Corinthians to covet to prophesy (1 Cor. xiv. 1, 39). When Christ pronounced John *to be Elias* (Matt. xi. 14), he declared that the Baptist had already attained to that spirit and power which the Essenes strove to obtain in their highest stage of purity.[7] It will therefore hardly be doubted that our Saviour himself belonged to this holy brotherhood. This will especially be apparent when we remember that the whole Jewish community, at the advent of Christ, was divided into three parties, the Pharisees, the Sadducees and the Essenes, and that every Jew had to belong to one of these sects. Jesus who, in all things, conformed to the Jewish law, and who was holy, harmless, undefiled, and separate from sinners, would therefore naturally associate himself with that order of Judaism which was most congenial to his holy nature. Moreover, the fact that Christ, with the exception of once, was not heard of in public till his thirtieth year, implying that he lived in seclusion with this fraternity, and that though he frequently rebuked the Scribes, Pharisees and Sadducees, he never denounced the Essenes, strongly confirms this conclusion. There can be no difficulty in admitting that the

7 For the passages embodying the sentiments of the Essenes, which constitute the above comparisons, we must refer to the second part of this Essay and the notes.

Saviour of the world, who taught us lessons from the sparrows
in the air, and the lilies in the field, and who made the whole
realm of nature tributary to his teachings, would commend
divine truth wherever it existed. But whilst Christ pro-
pounded some of the everlasting truths which were to be
found less adulterated and practised more conscientiously
among the Essenes than among the rest of the people, he
repudiated their extremes. They were ascetics; he ate and
drank the good things of God (Matt, xi. 19). They considered themselves defiled by contact with any one who
practised a lower degree of holiness than their own; Christ
associated with publicans and sinners, to teach them the way
to heaven. They sacrificed the lusts of their flesh to gain
spiritual happiness for themselves; Christ sacrificed himself
for the salvation of others.

It is now impossible to ascertain the precise date when
this order of Judaism first developed itself. According to
Philo, Moses himself instituted this order; Josephus contents
himself with saying that they existed " ever since the ancient
time of the fathers; " whilst Pliny assures us that, without
any one being born among them, the Essenes, incredible to
relate, have prolonged their existence for *thousands of ages.*"[8]
Bating, however, these assertions, which are quite in harmony
with the well known ancient custom of ascribing some pre-
Adamite period to every religious or philosophical system, it
must already have become apparent, from the description of
it, that the very nature of the Essenes precludes the possi-
bility of tracing its date. The fact that the Essenes developed themselves gradually, and at first imperceptibly, through
intensifying the prevalent religious notions, renders it impossible to say with exactness at what degree of intensity
they are to be considered as detached from the general body.

8 Compare the account of Philo, p. 36; Pliny, p. 40; Josephus, p. 52;
in the second part of this Essay.

The first mention we have of their existence is in the days of Jonathan the Maccabæan, B.C. 166. (*Joseph. Antiq.* xiii. 5, 8). We then hear of them again in the reign of Aristobulus I., B.C. 106, in connection with a prophecy about the death of Antigonus, uttered by Judas an Essene, of which Josephus gives the following account. "Judas, an Essene, whose predictions had up to this time never deceived, caused great astonishment on this occasion. When he saw at that time Antigonus pass through the temple, he called out to his disciples, of whom he had no small number—'Oh! it would be better for me to die now, since truth died before me, and one of my prophecies has proved false. Antigonus, who ought to have died this day, is alive; Strato's Tower, which is six hundred furlongs distance from here, is fixed for his murder, and it is already the fourth hour of the day [ten o'clock]; time condemns the prophecy as a falsehood.' Having uttered these words, the aged man sunk into a long, dejected, and sorrowing silence. Soon after, the report came that Antigonus was murdered in the subterranean passage which, like Cesarea on the sea side, was also called Strato's Tower. It was this circumstance that misled the prophet." (*Jewish War*, i. 3, § 5; *Antiq.* xiii. 11, § 2). The third mention of their existence we find in the well known prophecy of the Essene Manahem, uttered to Herod when a boy.[9] Now these accounts most unquestionably show that the Essenes existed at least two centuries before the Christian era, and that they at first lived amongst the Jewish community at large. Their residence at Jerusalem is also evident from the fact that there was a gate named after them ('Εσσηνῶν πύλη *Joseph. Jewish War*, v. 4, § 2). When they ultimately withdrew themselves from the rest of the Jewish nation, the majority of them settled on the north-west shore of the Dead Sea, sufficiently distant to escape its noxious exhalations, and the rest lived in scattered com-

9 This prophecy is given in full in the second part of this Essay, p. 50,

munities throughout Palestine and Syria. Both Philo and
Josephus estimated them to be above four thousand in number. This must have been exclusive of women and children.
We hear very little of them after this period (i.e. 40 A.D.) ;
and there can hardly be any doubt that, owing to the great
similarity which existed between their precepts and practices
and those of the primitive Christians, the Essenes as a body
must have embraced Christianity.

Having ascertained the character of the Essenes, we shall
be better prepared to investigate the origin of their name,
which has been the cause of so much controversy, and which
was not known even to Philo and Josephus. There is hardly
an expression the etymology of which has called forth such
a diversity of opinion as this name has elicited. The Greek
and the Hebrew, the Syriac and the Chaldee, names of persons
and names of places, have successively been tortured to con-
fess the secret connected with this appellation, and there are
no less, if not more, than *twenty different* explanations of it,
which I shall give in chronological order. Philo tells us that
some derived it from the Greek homonym ὁσιότης *holiness,*
because the Essenes were above all others worshippers of
God ; but he rejects it as incorrect (*vide infra, p.* 32) without
giving us another derivation. 2. Josephus does not expressly
give any derivation of it, but simply says, " the third sect who
really seem to practise holiness (ὁ δὴ καὶ δοκεῖ σεμνότητα ἀσκεῖν)
are called Essenes." *(Vide infra p.* 41*).* From the addition, however, " who really seem to practise holiness or piety,"
Frankel[10] argues that the word must mean *holiness* or *piety,*
because it appears to justify the name, and hence concludes
that Josephus most probably took it to be the Hebrew
חסידים or צנועים. Whilst Jost[11] is of opinion that Josephus
derived it from the Chaldee חשא *to be silent, to be mysterious,*

---

10 Zeitschrift für die religiösen Interessen des Judenthums. Berlin, 1856, p. 449.
11 Geschichte des Judenthums und seiner Secten, vol. 1. Leipzig, 1857, p. 207.

because חשן *the high priest's breast-plate*, for which the Septuagint has λογεῖον or λόγιον is translated by him ἐσσην, or that he might have deduced this idea from חשן itself, and traced it to λογεῖον or λόγιον as *endowed with the gift of prophecy.*[12] In Aboth of R. Nathan[13] it is written עשאני from עשה *to do, to perform*, and acccordingly denotes *the performers of the law.* 4. Epiphanius again calls them 'Οσσαῖοι and 'Οσσηνοι and tells us that it etymologically signifies στιβαρὸν γίνος *the stout* or *strong race*, evidently taking it for חסין or עזים. 5. In another place Epiphanius affirms that the Essenes borrowed their name from *Jesse* the father of David, or from *Jesus*, whose doctrines he ascribes to them; explaining the name Jesus to signify in Hebrew *a physician ;* and calls them *Jesseans.*[14] In this he is followed by Petitus who makes them so related to David that they were obliged to take the name of his father *Jesus* or *Jesse ;*[15] although Jesus does not signify physician but *God-help.* 6. Suidas *(Lex s. v.)* and Hilgenfeld *(Die jüdische Apokal. p.* 278*)*, make it out to be the form חזין = θεωρητικοί *seers*, and the latter maintains that this name was given to them because they pretended to see visions and to prophesy. 7. Josippon b. Gorion[16] *(lib.* iv. *sects.* 6, 7, *p.p.* 274 *and* 278, *ed. Breithaupt),* and

12 As Mr. Westcott, the writer of the article ESSENES in *Smith's Dictionary of the Bible*, has misunderstood this passage and wrongly represented Jost himself as deriving this name from חשון *the silent, the mysterious*, we give Jost's own words:—" Uns will scheinen, dass Josephus den Namen allerdings von חשה *schweigen, geheimnissvoll sein*, ableitet ; dahin führt seine Uebertragung des Wortes חשן in die griechischen Buchstaben ἐσσην Ed. Hav. Ant. 1, 147, welches Wort die LXX λογεῖον übersetzen. Da das Wort חשון seinen Zeitgenossen sehr geläufig war, so konnte er annehmen, dass man sich unter dem Namen der Sekte eiuen angemessenen Begriff dachte und er keiner Erläuterung bedürfe. Ja, es wäre möglich, dass er den Begriff aus חשן selbst ableitet, und auf λογεῖον oder λόγιον, als mit Weissagung begabte, zurückführte. Vergleichte Gfrörer, Philo 1, 196."

13 Aboth di. R. Nathan, cap. xxxvi.
14 Comp. Epiphan. Haeres. xix. lib. i. tom. ii. sect. 4, p. 120, ed. Petav.
15 Comp. Petite Variae Lectiones, c. xxviii. p. 2600.
16 *Josippon b. Gorion* also called *Gorionides*, lived in Italy about the middle of the tenth century. He is the compiler of the celebrated Hebrew Chronicle called *Jusippon*, or the Hebrew Josephus. His real character and the value of his Chronicle are discussed under the article JOSSIPPON in *Dr. Alexander's edition of Kitto's Cyclopædia of Biblical Literature.*

Gale *(Court of the Gentiles, part* ii., *p.* 147*)*, take it for the Hebrew חסידים *the pious, the puritans.* 8. De Rossi[17] *(Meor Enaim,* 82 *a)*, Gfrörer (Philo, ii. *p.* 341), Herzfeld *(Geschichte d. V. Israel* ii. *p.* 397*),* and others, insist that it is the Aramaic אסיא = δεραπευτής *physician,* and that this name was given to them because of the spiritual or physical cures they performed. Indeed, De Rossi and Herzfeld will have it that the sect *Baithusians* ביתוסים mentioned in the Talmud is nothing but a contraction of בית אסי *the school* or *sect of physicians,* just as כית הילל stands for *the school of Hillel.* 9. Salmasius affirms that the Essenes derived their name from the town called *Essa,* situated beyond the Jordan, which is mentioned by Josephus *(Antiq.* xiii. 15, § 2), or from the place *Vadi Ossis.*[18] 10. Rappaport *(Erech Milln, p.* 41), says that it is the Greek ἰσος *an associate, a fellow of the fraternity.* 11. Frankel *(Zeitschrift,* 1846, *p.* 449, &c.*),* and others think that it is the Hebrew expression צנועים *the retired.* 12. Ewald *(Geschichte d. Volkes Israel,* iv. *p.* 420*),* is sure that it is the Rabbinic חזן *servant (of God),* and that the name was given to them because it was their only desire to be δεραπευται δεοῦ. 13. Graetz *(Geschichte der Juden* iii. *p.* 468, *second ed.)* will have it that it is from the Aramaic סחא *to bathe,* with Aleph prostheticum, and that it is the shorter form for אסחאי צפרא = טובלי שחרית ἡμεροβαπτισται *hemerobaptists;* the Greek form 'Εσσαῖος, 'Εσσαῖοι being nothing but Assaï or Essaï with ה elided. 14. Dr. Löw *(Ben Chananja* vol. i. p. 352) never doubts but that they were called *Essenes* after their founder, whose name he tells us was ישי, the disciple of Rabbi Joshua ben Perachja. 15. Dr. Adler *(Volkslehrer,* vi. *p.* 50*),* again submits that it is from the

17 De Rossi, also called *Asarja min Ha-Adomim,* was born at Mantua in 1513, and died 1577. For an account of this eminent Jewish scholar, who may be regarded as the father of Biblical criticism at the time of the Reformation, see *Dr. Alexander's edition of Kitto's Cyclopædia of Biblical Literature,* Article Rossi.

18 Salmas. Plinian. exercitat. in Solinum cap. xxxv. p. 432, edit. Ultraject.

Hebrew אסר *to bind together, to associate*, and that they
were called אסרים because they united together to keep the
law.   16. Dr. Cohen suggests the Chaldee root עשׁן *to be
strong*, and that they were called עשׁיני because of their
strength of mind to endure sufferings and to subdue their
passions. *(Comp. Frankel's Monatschrift* viii. *p.* 272*).*
17. Oppenheim thinks that it may be the form עשׁין and stand
for עשׁין טהרת הקדשׁ or עשׁין טהרת חטאת *observers
of the laws of purity and holiness. (Ibid).*   18. Jellinek
(Ben Chananja iv. 374*)*, again derives it from the Hebrew
חצן *sinus,* περίζωμα, alluding to *the apron* which the Essenes
wore; whilst, 19, Others again derived it from חסיא *pious.*
The two last-mentioned explanations seem to have much to
recommend them, they are natural and expressive of the
characteristics of the brotherhood.   I, however, incline to
prefer the last, because it plainly connects the Essenes with
an ancient Jewish brotherhood called *Chassidim* חסידים *the
pious,* who preceded the Essenes, and from whom the latter
took their rise. Those who wish to trace this connection, will
find an article on *the Chassidim* in Dr. Alexander's edition of
KITTO'S CYCLOPÆDIA OF BIBLICAL LITERATURE.

II.

I shall now give in chronological order the description of the Essenes found in the writings of Philo, Pliny, Josephus, Solinus, Porphyry, Eusebius and Epiphanius, and subjoin such notes as will explain the difficulties, and show the historical value of the respective documents.

As Philo is the oldest in point of time, we will begin with him. The exact date of the birth of this celebrated Jewish-Alexandrian philosopher is not known. It is, however, generally agreed that he was born in Alexandria between the years 20 and 1 B.C., and died about 60 A.D. Having resided all his lifetime in Alexandria, his information about the Essenes, who lived in Palestine, was derived from hearsay. This will account for some of the inaccuracies in his description of this remarkable brotherhood. He has given us two accounts of them, one in his treatise, entitled *Every Virtuous Man is Free*, and the other in his treatise, called *Apology for the Jews*. The latter is no longer extant, but Eusebius has preserved the fragments which speak of the Essenes in his work, entitled *Præparatio Evangelica* viii. 11. The description of the so-called contemplative Essenes, or Therapeutæ, which is generally appealed to as illustrating the doctrines and practices of the brotherhood in question, has nothing whatever to do with the real Palestinian Essenes; and it is almost certain that it is one of the many apocryphal productions fathered upon Philo, as may be seen from Graetz's elaborate and masterly analysis of it.[1] Philo's first account is contained in his treatise entitled *Every Virtuous Man is Free*, and is as follows :[2]

1 Comp. Graetz, Geschichte der Juden. Dritter Band, Zweite Auflage, Leipzig. 1863, p. 464, &c.; Frankel, Programm des jüdisch-theol. Seminars von 1854.

2 Comp. Philonis Opera, ed. Mangey. London, 1742, vol. ii. pp. 457–45.

" Palestine, and Syria too, which are inhabited by no slight portion of the numerous population of the Jews, are not barren of virtue. There are some among them called Essenes ('Εσσαῖοι),—in number more than four thousand,—from, as I think, an incorrect derivation from the Greek homonym *hosiotes*, holiness (παρώνυμοι ὁσιότητος), because they are above all others worshippers of God (Ξεραπευταὶ Ξεοῦ). They do not sacrifice any animals, but rather endeavour to make their own minds fit for holy offering (ἱεροπρεπεῖς διανοίας).[3] They, in the first place, live in villages, avoiding cities on account of the habitual wickedness of the citizens, being sensible that as disease is contracted from breathing an impure atmosphere, so an incurable impression is made on the soul in such evil company.[4] Some of them cultivate the earth, others are engaged in those diverse arts which promote peace, thus

3 Josephus, who also mentions this fact, distinctly says that their not offering sacrifices in the temple is owing to the different degree of holiness which they practised. (*Vide infra p.* 228.) From the repeated declarations in the Bible, that a life of uniform obedience and faithful service is far more acceptable to God than the cattle of a thousand hills (1 Sam. xv. 22 ; Ps. xl. 7 ; l. 7–14 ; li. 17 ; Prov. xxxi. 3 ; Isa. i. 11, 17 ; lxv. 3 ; Jer. vii. 21–23 ; Hos. vi. 6 ; xiv. 3 ; Micah, vi. 6–8), the Essenes could easily be reconciled to their abstaining from offering animal sacrifices, and would be led to attach infinitely greater importance to the presenting of their bodies a living sacrifice, holy and acceptable to God. (Comp. also Rom. xii. 1). This circumstance led Petitius to the conclusion that Herod, who was friendly to the Essenes in consequence of the favorable prophecy about him uttered by the Essene Menahem *(vide infra p.* 50), employed them to translate the Prophets and the Psalms into Greek, and that they availed themselves of the opportunity to introduce their tenets and rites into this version, now called the Septuagint. Thus, for instance, when David said " Sacrifice and burnt offering thou didst not desire, mine ears hast thou opened " (Ps. xl. 6), the Essenes rendered it " Sacrifice and burnt offering thou dost not desire, but a body hast thou prepared me," interpolating three of their tenets. 1. They made the Prophet speak absolutely, as if God had entirely rejected sacrifices because they would offer him none. 2. By dropping the words, "*mine ears hast thou opened,*" they showed their disapprobation of slavery. (Comp. Exod. xxi). And 3, by substituting "*a body* hast thou prepared me," they understood the college of devout Essenes, who met together as a body, and whom God appointed instead of sacrifice. Comp. Basnage, History of the Jews, English translation. London, 1708, p. 128.

4 This is not the only reason why the Essenes withdrew from cities. Their observance of the Levitical laws of purity which rendered them impure when they came in contact with those who did not live according to the same rules, was the principal cause of their living separately. (*Vide supra p.* 7, *note* 1.) Philo, however, states the first reason because the Greeks, for whom he wrote, understood it better than the second, which is so peculiarly Jewish in its character.

benefitting themselves and their neighbours. They do not lay up treasures of gold or silver,[5] nor do they acquire large portions of land out of a desire for revenues, but provide themselves only with the absolute necessities of life. Although they are almost the only persons of all mankind who are without wealth and possessions—and this by their own choice rather than want of success—yet they regard themselves as the richest, because they hold that the supply of our wants, and contentment of mind, are riches, as in truth they are.[6]

"No maker of arrows, darts, spears, swords, helmets, breast-plates, or shields—no manufacturer of arms or engines of war, nor any man whatever who makes things belonging to war, or even such things as might lead to wickedness in times of peace, is to be found among them.[7] Traffic, innkeeping, or navigation, they never so much as dream of, because they repudiate every inducement to covetousness. There is not a single slave to be found among them, for all are free, and mutually serve each other. They condemn owners of slaves, not only as unjust, inasmuch as they corrupt the principle of equality, but also as impious, because they destroy the law of nature, which like a mother brought forth and nourished all alike, and made them all legitimate brethren, not only in word but in deed ; but this relationship, treacherous covetousness, rendered overbearing by success, has destroyed by engendering enmity instead of cordiality, and hatred instead of love.

"They leave the logical part of philosophy, as in no respect necessary for the acquisition of virtue, to the word catchers ; and the natural part, as being too difficult for human nature, to the astrological babblers, excepting that part of it which treats upon the existence of God and the origin of the

5 The same thing Christ urged on his disciples. Comp. Matth. vi. 19–21.

6 This simple desire for the supply of our daily bread, and the contentment of mind here spoken of, are also commended by our Saviour. (Matth. vi. 11, 25–34.)

7 Believing that all they that take the sword shall perish with the sword. Comp. Matth. xxvi. 52.

C

universe;[8] but the ethical part they thoroughly work out themselves, using as their guides the laws which their fathers inherited, and which it would have been impossible for the human mind to devise without divine inspiration. Herein they instruct themselves at all times, but more especially on the seventh day. ˙For the seventh day is held holy, on which they abstain from all other work, and go to the sacred places called synagogues, sit according to order, the younger below the elder, and listen with becoming attention. Then one takes the Bible and reads it, and another of those who have most experience comes forward and expounds it, passing over that which is not generally known, for they philosophise on most things in symbols according to the ancient zeal.

"They are instructed in piety, holiness, righteousness, economy, politics, in knowledge of what is truly good, bad and indifferent, to choose things that are necessary, and to avoid the contrary. They use therein a threefold rule and definition, viz.: love of God, love of virtue, and love of mankind.[9] Of their love to God, they give innumerable demonstrations—e.g. their constant and unalterable holiness (ἁγνεία) throughout the whole of their life; their avoidance of oaths[10] and falsehoods, and their firm belief that God is the source of all good, but of nothing evil. Of their love of virtue they give proofs in their contempt for money, fame, and pleasures,

8 The Apostle Paul, too, admonished the Colossians to "beware lest any man spoil you through philosophy." (Col. ii. 8.)

9 Thus also Christ, when he was asked which was the greatest commandment in the law, declared, love to God and love to our neighbour, and that on these two hang all the law and the prophets. (Comp. Matth. xxii. 36–40.)

10 Although the taking of oaths was discountenanced by the Jews generally (Comp. Ecclus. xxiii. 11, &c.; and especially Philo De decem oraculis § 17, Opp. Tom. ii. p. 194, &c., ed. Mangey); and the Pharisees took great care to abstain as much as possible from using them (Comp. Shevuoth 39, b; Gittin 35, a; Bemidbar Rabba c. xxii); yet the Essenes were the only order who laid it down as a principle not to swear at all, but to say yea, yea, and nay, nay. So firmly and conscientiously did they adhere to it that Herod, who on ascending the throne had exacted an oath of allegiance from all the rest of the Jews, was obliged to absolve the Essenes from it. (Comp. Joseph. Antiq. book xv. chap. x. § 4). Christ too, laid it down as a principle for his disciples not to swear at all, but to say yea, yea, and nay, nay. (Comp. Matth. v. 33–37.)

their continence, endurance, in their satisfying their wants easily, simplicity, cheerfulness of temper, modesty, order, firmness, and every thing of the kind. As instances of their love to man, are to be mentioned their benevolence, equality, and their having all things in common, which is beyond all description, and about which it will not be out of place to speak here a little.

"First, then, no one has his own house, so that it also belongs to all. For, besides that, they all live together in sodalities; it is also open to those of the brotherhood who come from other places. Moreover, they have all one common treasury and store of provisions, common garments, and common food for all who eat together. Such a mode of sleeping together, living together, and eating together, could not be so easily established in fact among any other people; and indeed it would be impossible. For whatever they receive daily, if they work for wages, they do not retain it as their own, but give it to the common stock, and let every one that likes make common use of it.[11] Those that are sick are not neglected because they can earn nothing, but have what is necessary for their aid from the common stock, so that they ever fare richly without wanting anything. They manifest respect, reverence and care for the aged, just as children do for their parents, administering to them a thousand times with all plentifulness both with their hands and their counsels in their old age.

"Such champions of virtue does a philosophy produce which is free from the subtlety of Greek word-splitting, and which deals with subjects tending to the exercise of praiseworthy actions, and giving rise to invincible freedom. This was seen in the fact that many tyrants have arisen from time to time in that country, differing in character and conduct.

---

11 This community of goods was also adopted by the early Christians, who, as we are told, "sold their possessions and goods, and parted them to all as every man needed."—(Comp. Acts, ii. 45, iv. 34, 35.)

Some of them endeavoured to surpass in ferocity wild beasts; they omitted no manner of barbarity, they sacrificed the vanquished in whole troops, or, like butchers, cut off pieces and limbs of those that were still living, and did not leave off till retributive justice, which governs the affairs of man, plunged them into similar miseries. Others, again, converted their frenzy and madness into a different kind of wickedness. They adopted an inexpressible bitterness, spake gently, and betrayed a ferocious temper under the mask of gentle language;[12] they fawned like poisonous dogs, and brought about irremediable miseries, leaving behind them in the cities, as monuments of their impiety and hatred of mankind, the never to be forgotten miseries. But neither the cruel tyrant nor the wily hypocrite could get any advantage over the said brotherhood of Essenes or *holy ones* ('Εσσαίων ἤ ὁσίων), but disarmed by the virtues of these men, all recognised them as independent and free by nature, praised their common meals and their community of goods, which surpasses all description, and is an evident proof of a perfect and very happy life."

Philo's second account, which has been preserved by Eusebius in his *Praep. Evàng.*, viii, 11, from the lost treatise entitled *Apology for the Jews*, is as follows :—[13]

"Our lawgiver, Moses, formed innumerable (μυρίους) disciples into a fellowship called Essenes,[14] who, as it appears, obtained this appellation by virtue of their holiness (παρὰ τὴν ὁσιότητα). They dwell in many cities of Judea, and in villages, and

12 The account here given of the sufferings of the Essenes bears a very striking resemblance to the description in *the Epistle to the Hebrews* xi. 36-38; and it may be that the Apostle refers to this extraordinary brotherhood.

13 This fragment which Eusebius has preserved is given in Philo's Works, ed. Mangey, vol. ii., p, 622, *seq.*

14 The tracing of this brotherhood to Moses is in accordance with the practice which generally prevailed among the Jews of ascribing the origin of every law, mystical doctrine or system, which came into vogue in the course of time, either to Ezra, Moses, Noah or Adam. Thus we are told in the Jerusalem Talmud (Pea, ii. 6), and the Midrash (*Coheleth*, 96 *d.*), that all the Scriptural learning which developed itself in course of time, and everything which a *Talmid Vatic* might bring to light, were revealed to Moses beforehand on Mount Sinai.

in large and populous communities. Their order is not
founded upon natural descent, but upon admiration for virtue
and sincere love for man. Hence there are properly speaking
no newly born ones among the Essenes, no children, no
youths, as the dispositions of these are unstable and liable to
change from the imperfections incident to their age ;[15] but they
are all full grown men who are already approaching old age ;
and are no longer carried away by the impetuosity of their
bodily passions, but possess the genuine and the only true and
real liberty. A proof of their freedom is to be found in their
life. None of them strives to acquire any private property,
house, slave, farm, flocks, herds, or anything which might
be regarded as a source of riches, but they all give everything
to the common stock from which the common wants of all are
alike supplied.

" They all dwell together in the same place, form themselves
into companies, societies, combinations and unions,[16] and work
together all their life for the common good of the brotherhood.
The different members of the order are engaged in different
employment ; they work cheerfully and industriously, and
never try to leave their employment on account of cold, heat,
or any change of weather. They go to their daily work before
the sun rises, and do not leave off till some time after it has
set, when they return home rejoicing no less than those who
have been exercising themselves in gymnastic contests.[17] They
believe that their employment is a sort of gymnastic exercise
·of more benefit to life, greater pleasure both to soul and
body, and of a more enduring advantage than any mere
athletic labours, because they can cheerfully continue in their

15 This refers to juvenile *members of the fraternity*, as the Essenes did adopt
children, and trained them up to the practices of the order. *Vide infra p.* 41.

16 The four companies here mentioned most probably refer to the four
different classes into which the Essenes were divided, described more minutely
by Josephus. *Vide infra*, p. 47, note 45.

17 So also the Apostle Paul recommends us not to be slothful in business, but
fervent in spirit, serving the Lord.—(Rom. xii. 11.)

work as a recreation even when youth and bodily strength are gone. Those who are acquainted with the cultivation of the land are engaged in agriculture; others, again, who understand the management of animals, attend to the flocks; some are skilful in the management of bees; and others again, are artizans and manufacturers, thus guarding against the want of anything. They do not omit anything which is requisite to supply the absolute necessities of life.

"The appointed steward and general manager receives the wages which the different people get for their respective employments, and forthwith buys plenty of food and other necessaries of life. They eat at the same table, and have every day the same food, being lovers of frugality and moderation, and averse to luxury and extravagance as a disease of both mind and body. Not only is their table in common, but their dress too is in common. They have a store of rough cloaks in the winter, and in the summer cheap garments without sleeves, to which every one can go and freely take whichever kind he wants, for whatever belongs to one belongs to all, and whatever belongs to all belongs to each individual.

"If one of them is sick, he is cured from the common resources, and is attended to by the general care and anxiety of the whole body. The old men, even if they happen to be childless,[18] end their lives in a most happy, prosperous and tenderly cared for old age, as if they were not only the fathers of many children, but were even also particularly happy in an affectionate offspring. They are looked upon by such a number of people as worthy of so much honour and provident regard, that they think themselves bound to care for them even more from inclination than from any tie of natural affection.

"Perceiving, with more than ordinary acuteness and accuracy, what is alone, or at least above all other things, calculated

18 That is if he belongs to the class of Essenes who practised celibacy; for there were those among them who had wives and families. *Vide infra p. 49.*

to dissolve such connections, they repudiate marriage; and at the same time practice continence in an eminent degree. For no one of the Essenes marries a wife, because woman is a selfish and excessively jealous creature, and has great power to destroy the morals of man, and to mislead with continual tricks; for she is always devising flattering speeches and other kinds of hypocrisy as on a stage; bewitching the eyes and the ears; and when they are subjugated like things stultified, she proceeds to undermine the ruling intellect.[19]

"But when she has children, the woman becomes full of pride and arrogance, audaciously speaks out that which she previously merely indicated in treacherous disguise, and without any shame compels one to do whatever is hostile to the brotherhood; for he who is chained by the charms of a woman or cares for children by necessity of nature, is no longer the same person to others, but is entirely changed, having unawares become a slave instead of a free man.

19 The Mosaic law regards conjugal intercourse as polluting, and enjoins bathing after it. (Levit. xv. 18.) Hence, when the children of Israel had to sanctify themselves in the highest degree, so as to be fit to receive the law from Mount Sinai, they were commanded not to approach their wives (Exod. xix. 15). Hence, also, those who had the charge of the shew-bread polluted the sacred loaves by going to their wives (1 Sam. xxi. 4). And hence the remark of the Apostle Paul, that in order to give themselves to fasting and prayer, man and wife may keep aloof from each other by mutual consent (1 Cor. vii. 5). The same laws obtained among all nations of antiquity. Thus, among the Egyptians, Babylonians, Arabians, Greeks and Romans, both man and wife had to bathe after connubial intercourse (*Herod.* i. 198). No one was allowed to go after it to the temple without bathing (*Herod.* ii. 64; *Suet. Aug.* xciv. 5; *Pers.* ii. 50, &c.); and the priests had to abstain from approaching their wives when they were ministering in holy things (*Porphyrius, de Abstinentia,* lib. ii. 50; iv. 7; *Plutarch. Sympos.* iii. 6; *Tibul.* lib. ii. Eleg. 1, 11, &c.; *Ovid. Metam.* x. 434, &c.) Now, as the Essenes strove to be in a perpetual state of sanctification, regarded their refectory as a sanctuary and their meals as sacraments, and most anxiously avoided contact with every thing that defiled, they had of necessity to extend these Mosaic laws, which enjoin abstinence from connubial intercourse as a means of sanctification, and which regard those who indulged in it as defiled, to the whole course of their life; and they had therefore to be celibates. This extension of the Mosaic law was moreover deemed desirable in consequence of the general conviction which the Jews entertained, in common with other nations, that no woman remains faithful to her husband, and that they all defile the bed of marriage. Philo, in the passage before us, and Josephus, as we shall see afterwards (*vide infra p.* 41, § 2), only give the latter reason, to suit their Greek readers who could both understand it better and sympathise with it more than with the former.

" Such is the enviable system of life of the Essenes, so that not only private individuals but even mighty kings have admired them, venerated their brotherhood, and rendered their dignity and nobleness still higher by the praise and honours which they lavished upon them."

Next, in point of time, is Caius Plinius Secundus, called Major, or the elder, the celebrated author of the *Historia Naturalis*, who was born in A.D. 23, and died A.D. 79. Pliny's notice of the Essenes, which is to be found in his Natural History, book v., chap. xvii., is as follows :

" Towards the west [of the sea] and sufficiently distant from it, so as to escape its noxious exhalations *(ab occidente litora Esseni fugiunt, usque qua nocent)*, are the Essenes. They are a hermitical society, marvellous beyond all others throughout the whole earth. They live without any women, without gratifying sensual desires, without money, and in the company of palm trees. Their ranks are daily made up by multitudes of new comers who resort to them ; and who being weary of life, and driven by the surges of ill-fortune, adopt their manner of life. Thus it is that, through thousands of ages (*per saeculorum millia*),[20] incredible to relate, this people prolongs its existence without any one being born among them : so fruitful to them are the weary lives of others."

Next in point of time is Josephus, or Joseph ben Matthias, better known by the name Flavius Josephus, who was born in Jerusalem about 37, A.D. The description which this learned Jewish warrior and historian gives us of the Essenes, although somewhat marred by being made to harmonise with the systems of Greek philosophy, is very important, inasmuch as Josephus was not only a Palestinian Jew, but at one period of his life had actually joined the brotherhood. He tells us in his autobiography, that when sixteen years old he determined to

20 This is simply a repetition of what the Essenes themselves said about their origin, in accordance with a common practice among the Jews.—*Vide supra p. 36, note* 14.

examine for himself the respective merits of the three predominant sects, viz., of the Pharisees, Sadducees and Essenes, with the view of making a selection from among them. His accounts of the Essenes are dispersed through his works. The following is the first description contained in his *Jewish War*, book ii, chap. viii, sec. 2—13.

"§ 2. There are three sects of philosophers among the Jews. The followers of the first are called Pharisees, of the second Sadducees, and of the third, who really seem to practise holiness, Essenes.[21] Jews by birth, they love each other more than the others.[22] They reject pleasure as an evil, and regard continence and not yielding to passions as virtues. They despise marriage, and adopt the children of others while still tender and susceptible of instruction,[23] and regard them as their own relations, and train them in their practices. They do not, however, repudiate marriage, and its consequent succession of the race in themselves; but they are afraid of the lasciviousness of women, and are persuaded that none of them preserve their fidelity to one man.[24]

"§ 3. They despise riches, have all things in common in a very admirable manner, and there is not one to be found among them who is richer than another; for it is a law that those who enter the sect must give up their possessions to the

21 This representation of the three Jewish sects as different philosophical schools, and the supposed resemblance of the Essenes to the Pythagoreans, which he mentions afterwards, (*vide infra Antiq.* xv. 10; § 4, p. 50) and which have misled modern writers, are nothing but a desire on the part of Josephus to make the divers teachings of his co-religionists correspond to the different systems of Greek philosophy. It is this anxiety to shew the Gentiles, for whom he wrote, how much the Jews resemble them both in doctrine and practice, which detracts from the merits of Josephus' history.

22 This love for the brotherhood, which the Essenes possessed to so extraordinary a degree, was also urged by the Evangelists and Apostles on the early Christians (comp. John xiv. 17; Rom. xiii. 8; 1 Tim. iv. 9; 1 Peter i. 28; xi. 17; 1 John iii. 23; iv. 7, 11; v. 2).

23 This does not contradict Philo's remark (*vide supra* p. 37), as Herzfeld supposes, (*Geschichte des Volkes Israel*, vol ii. p. 375); since the two statements refer to two different things. The former affirms that they do not receive children into the noviciate, whilst the latter speaks of their adopting and educating them, which is a distinct thing from *becoming a novice*.

24 *Vide supra, p.* 39, *note* 19.

society as common property,[25] so that there is not to be seen among them all, either the abjectness of poverty or the distinction of riches; but as every man's goods are cast into a common treasury, they all, like brothers, have one patrimony. They regard ointment as defiling; and if one happens to be anointed against his will, he immediately wipes it off his body.[26] To be unadorned but dressed in white they regard as commendable. They have stewards of their common property, appointed by general election, and every one without distinction is proposed for all the offices.

"§ 4. They have no separate city, but some of them live anywhere; and if any of the society come from other places, whatever they have lies open for them, just as if it were their own; and they go to those whom they have never seen before as if they had been most intimate. Hence they take nothing with them when they go on a journey,[27] but arms for defence against robbers. A steward is appointed in every city of this order to provide strangers with clothes and other necessaries.[28] The keeping and appearance of their body are such as of children brought up in fear; they change neither garments nor shoes till they are worn out or made unfit by time.[29] They neither sell nor buy anything among themselves, but everyone gives of that which he has to him that wants, and gets from

25 So our Lord urged on the young man, who lived so exemplary a life in the performance of God's law, and whom he loved, that unless he gave up his property he could not follow him (comp. Matth. xix. 21; Mark x. 21; Luke xviii. 22), and commanded his disciples to sell all their possessions and distribute the money among the poor (comp. Luke xii. 33.)

26 Ointment being a luxury (comp. Eccl. ix. 8; Dan. x. 2), the Essenes regarded the use of it as extravagance, and contrary to the simplicity of their manner of life.

27 The manner in which Christ commanded his disciples to depart on their journey (Mark vi. 8-10) is the same which these pious Essenes are here said to have adopted. This also explains the injunction given by our Saviour to his disciples in Luke xxii. 36, about taking arms with them, which has so greatly perplexed commentators who were unacquainted with the customs of the Essenes.

28 The Pharisees, too, had a steward in every place to supply the needy with clothing and food. (Comp. Pea viii. 7; Baba Bathra 8 a; Sabbath 118.)

29 Comp. also Luke x. 4, &c.

him that which he needs; and even without requital they can freely take whatever they want.

"§ 5. Their piety towards God is extraordinary, for they never speak about worldly matters before the sun rises, but offer up, with their faces towards it, some of the prayers transmitted by their forefathers, as if they supplicated it to rise.[30] Hereupon, they are all sent by the overseers, every one to work in the department in which he is skilled; and, having diligently laboured till the fifth hour, assemble again together in one place, girt round with their linen apron, and have a baptism with cold water.[31] After this lustration they resort to a special house, in which no one of another faith is admitted, and go to the refectory purified as into a holy temple.[32] Having quietly taken their seats the baker gives every one a loaf of bread according to order, and the cook places before each one a dish with one sort of food. The priest commences with prayer, and no one is allowed to taste his food before grace is said. He also returns thanks after the meal; for both at the commencement and at the conclusion they praise God as the giver of their food.[33]

30 Some translate it "they offer prayer (εἰς τὸν ἥλιον) to the sun." But it is utterly inconceivable that the Essenes, who were such thorough Jews, and so exemplary for their adoration of the Holy One of Israel, would be guilty of idolatry by worshipping the sun. Besides, the prayer in question is described as one transmitted by the fathers. And can it be imagined that there existed among the Jews a national prayer to this luminary in direct violation of the first commandment, and of what is so expressly forbidden in Deut. iv. 10? The prayer therefore here spoken of is the well known national morning hymn of praise (המאיר לאיש) for the return of the light of the day, which still forms a part of the Jewish service to the present day. Comp Berachoth 9 b; Rappaport in the Bikure Ha-Ittim, vol. x., Vienna 1829, p. 115, and infra p. 69.

31 This practice of bathing before meals was also common among the Pharisees (comp. Chagiga, 18, b), and as the Essenes covered themselves with their aprons so the Pharisees put on their Talith during their baptisms. (Comp. Berachoth 24, b.)

32 The Pharisees, too, regarded the refectory as a sanctuary, and compared its table to the altar in the temple, because the altar in the temple is represented as the table of the Lord (Ezekiel xli, 22). Hence, R. Jochanan and R. Eleazar remark—"As long as the temple stood the altar atoned for the sins of Israel, but now it is man's table which atones for his sins." (Talmud Berachoth, 55a). Hence the Chaldee paraphrase of Ezekiel xii. 22, and the remarks of Rashi and Kimchi on this passage, which cannot be understood unless this traditional interpretation is borne in mind. Comp. also Aboth iii, 3.

33 This was also the practice of the Pharisees, and is to the present day the custom among the orthodox Jews.

Whereupon they put off their white garments as if they were sacred, and betake themselves again to their work till evening. On returning again they take their supper together, at which strangers, who happen to be in the place, are allowed to sit down with them. No noise or tumult ever desecrates their house, but they let every one take part in the conversation in turn ; and the silence of those who are within appears to those that are without as some awful mystery. The cause of this is the uninterrupted sobriety, as well as the fact that their eating and drinking are so measured out as just to suffice the cravings of nature.

"§ 6. Whilst they do nothing without the injunctions of their overseers, yet there are two things in which they have free action, viz., helping the needy, and shewing mercy ; to help the deserving when they are in want, and to give food to the hungry, they have perfect liberty ; but to give anything to their relations they are not allowed without the permission of the overseers. They are just dispensers of their anger, curbers of their passions, representatives of fidelity, ministers of peace ; and every word with them is of more force than an oath. They avoid taking an oath, and regard it as worse than perjury ; for they say that he who is not believed without calling on God to witness is already condemned of falsehood.[34] They take extraordinarily great pains in studying the writings of the ancients, and select that especially which is beneficial both for the soul and body ; hence they investigate medical roots and the property of minerals for the cure of distempers.[35]

"§ 7. When any one desires to enter the sect, he is not immediately admitted, but although he has to remain a whole

[34] This paragraph almost embodies the sentiments uttered by our Saviour in Matth. chap. v.

[35] These ancient books on magical cures and exorcisms were the reputed works of Solomon, who, according to the Talmud as well as the Byzantine and Arabian writers, composed treatises on miraculous cures and driving out evil spirits. (*Comp. Pesachim* 56 a; *Fabricius, Codex pseudepigraphus Vet. Test. p.* 1042, &c.; *Weil, Bibliblische Legenden der Muselmänner, p.* 225–279). Josephus tells

year without, yet he is obliged to observe their ascetic rules
of living, and they give him an axe, an apron as mentioned
above, and a white garment.[36] If he has given proof of continence during this time, he approaches nearer to their life
and partakes of the holier water of purification ; but is
still not as yet admitted to their common table. Having
thus given proof of his perseverance, his conduct is tested
two more years, and, if found worthy, he is admitted into the
society. But before he touches the common meal, he swears,
by most awful oaths,[37] first to fear God, and next to exercise
justice towards all men—neither to wrong any one of his
own accord nor by the command of others ; always to detest
the wicked and side with the righteous ; ever to keep faith
inviolable with all men, especially with those in authority,
for no one comes to office without the will of God ;[38] not
to be proud of his power nor to outshine his subordinates,
either in his garments or greater finery, if he himself should

us elsewhere that some of these Solomonic productions still existed in his
own days, and that he had actually seen demons driven out and people
cured by their aid. (*Comp. Antiq.* book viii. chap. ii. § 5.) This account most
strikingly illustrates what Christ says in Matth. xii. 27.

36 This custom has its origin in the extension of a Mosaic law. The hosts
of the Lord are commanded in Deut. xxiii 13, 15, to have spades among the
martial instruments in order to bury therewith their excrements without the camp,
and thus to keep themselves pure from every pollution, and to be a holy camp,
because the Holy One of Israel dwells in the midst thereof. Now as the Essenes
strove to be, in a pre-eminent sense, the spiritual hosts of the Lord, every one of
them was obliged to have this spade in order to guard their sacred camp from
defilement. For this reason the apron was also given to cover their nakedness in
their numerous baptisms, and thus to keep their thoughts from dwelling upon
anything which might lead to impurity ; whilst the white garment was the symbol
of their holiness. This, however, was not peculiar to the Essenes, as the Talmud
tells us that when any one applied to become a member of the Pharisaic order
(חבר), he had to pass through a noviciate of twelve months, at the expiration of
which he received a sort of garment called כנסים, and having duly qualified himself in this stage, he was afterwards admitted to the holier lustrations (מקבלין
לכנסים ואחר כד מקבלין למהרות). (*Comp. Tosifta Demai e.* 11 ; *Jerusalem Demai*
ii. 3 ; *Babylonian Becharoth* 30, 6).

37 This was the only occasion on which the Essenes were permitted to take an
oath.

38 This does not refer to governments generally, as Gfrörer will have it (*Philo
und die jüdisch-alexandrinische Theosophie*, vol. ii, p. 333, &c.), but to the office
of overseer or steward *among the brotherhood*, as is evident from the immediately
following statement, which most unquestionably pledges every Essene to retain
his simplicity of character if he should ever attain to any official position or
stewardship in the order.

attain to office ; always to love truth and strive to reclaim all
liars ; to keep his hands clear from stealing, and his mind
from unholy gain ; not to conceal anything from the brotherhood, nor disclose anything belonging to them to those
without, though it were at the hazard of his life. He has,
moreover, to swear not to communicate to any one their
doctrines in any other way than he has received them ;[39] to
abstain from robbing the commonwealth ; and equally to
preserve the writings of the society and the names of the
angels.[40] By such oaths they bind those who enter the brotherhood.

"§ 8. Such as are caught in heinous sins are excommunicated
from the society ; and the excommunicated frequently die a
miserable death. For, being bound by oaths and customs,
they cannot receive food from any out of the society, so that
they are forced to eat herbs till, their bodies being famished
with hunger, they perish.[41] Hence they compassionately receive many of them again when they are at their last gasp,
thinking that suffering, approaching unto death, is sufficient
for their sins.

"§ 9. In their verdicts they are most exact and just, and
never give sentence if there are less than a hundred of the

39 This is not peculiar to the Essenes. The Pharisees, too, would not indis-
criminately propound the mysteries of the cosmogony and the theosophy, which,
according to them, are contained in the history of the Creation and in the vision
of Ezekiel, except to those who were regularly initiated in the order. Comp.
Mishna Chagiga, ii, 1.

40 This evidently refers to the secrets of the *Tetragrammaton*, and the ange-
lology which played so important a part among the Jewish mystics from time
immemorial. Comp. Wisdom of Solomon vii. 20 ; Mishna Chagiga, ii, 1.

41 The reason why he ate herbs and not bread, or the simple dish which the
order generally took, is that, being bound by an oath to observe the practices of
the brotherhood, he could only accept meals from those who lived according to the
highest degree of purity (על מהרת וחמאת), and who, as a matter of course, kept
their meals according to this degree. But as such a mode of life was of very
uncommon occurrence, the excommunicated Essene was obliged to live on herbs
or vegetables which he had to pluck himself; for, according to the Talmud,
plants are only then considered unclean when they are *cut off* and water is poured
upon them (משהוכשרו לקבל טומאה משנתלשו). As for Josephus' saying that he
died a miserable death, and that he could only eat *grass* (ποιηφάγων), this is
simply another instance of his exaggerating and colouring his subject.

brotherhood present : but what is then decreed is irrevocable. Next to God they have the highest veneration for the name of the lawgiver, Moses, and punish with death any one who blasphemes it. To submit to the elders and to the majority they regard as a duty : hence, when ten of them sit together, no one will speak if the other nine do not agree to it. They avoid spitting before the face, or to the right hand,[42] and are also stricter than all other Jews not to touch any labour on the Sabbath day—for they not only prepare their Sabbath-day's food the day before, that they may not kindle a fire on that day, but they will not move a vessel out of its place[43] nor go to ease nature. On all other days they dig a pit of a foot deep with the spade (such an one being given to the novice), and having covered it all round with a cover, that it may not offend the Divine rays, they set themselves over it, and then put the earth that was dug out again into the pit; and do this, after having chosen the most lonely places. And although the voiding of bodily excrements is natural, yet it is their custom to bathe after it, as if they had been defiled.[44]

" § 10. They are divided, according to the time of leading this mode of life, into four different classes, and the juniors are so much inferior to the seniors, that the latter must wash themselves when they happen to touch the former, as if they had been defiled by a stranger.[45] They live to a great age, so

42 The Pharisees, too, regarded ten persons as constituting a complete number for divine worship, held the assembling of such a number as sacred, and would not spit in their presence. (*Comp. Berachoth* 54 a ; *Jerusalem Berachoth* iii. 5 ; *Aboth* iii. 6.)

43 This is not peculiar to the Essenes ; for the Pharisees, too, would not remove a vessel on the Sabbath (comp. *Tosifta Succa*, iii) ; and the orthodox Jews, to the present day, will not even carry a handkerchief on the Sabbath ; they tie it round the body to serve as a girdle, so that it might not be said that they carry the weight of even so small a thing on the sacred day. Comp. also Mark xi, 16.

44 Neither is this peculiar to the Essenes ; for not only did the Pharisees of old do the same (comp. *Ioma* 28, a) ; but the orthodox Jews of the present day wash after performing the duties of nature.

45 This division of the brotherhood into four classes, as well as the impurity contracted by the higher class when touching one who belonged to a lower class of purity, also existed among the Pharisees. (*Vide supra*, p. 7, note 1.)

that many of them live to above a hundred years—arising from the simplicity of their diet, as it appears to me, and from their order. They despise suffering, and overcome pain by fortitude. Death, if connected with honour, they look upon as better than long life. Of the firmness of their minds in all cases the war with the Romans has given ample proof; in which, though they were tortured, racked, burned, squeezed, and subjected to all the instruments of torment, that they might be forced to blaspheme the lawgiver or eat what was forbidden, yet they could not be made to do either of them; nor would they even once flatter their tormentors or shed a tear, but, smiling through their torments and mocking their tormentors, they cheerfully yielded up their souls, as those who would soon receive them back again.[46]

" § 11. For they firmly believe that the bodies perish and their substance is not enduring, but that the souls are immortal—continue for ever and come out of the most subtile ether —are enveloped by their bodies, to which they are attracted through a natural inclination, as if by hedges—and that when freed from the bonds of the body, they, as if released from a long servitude, rejoice and mount upwards. In harmony with the opinion of the Greeks,[47] they say that for the good souls there is a life beyond the ocean, and a region which is never molested either with showers or snow or intense heat—is always refreshed with the gentle gales of wind constantly breathing from the ocean; whilst to the wicked souls they assign a dark and cold corner, full of never-ceasing punishments. And it seems to be according to the same opinion that the Greeks assigned to their valiant men, whom they called heroes and demigods, the Island of the Blessed, but to the souls of the wicked the regions of the impious in Hades;

46 Philo, too, speaks of this fact. (*Vide supra p.* 86.)

47 This is another instance of the anxiety of Josephus to make the different phases of Judaism harmonise with the Greek mode of thinking.

as also their fables speak of several there punished, as Sisy-
phus and Tantalus and Ixion and Tityus. This they teach,
partly because they believe that the souls are immortal, and
partly for the encouragement of virtue and the discouragement
of vice. For good men are made better in their lives by the
hope of reward after their death, whilst the passions of the
wicked are restrained by the fear they are in that, although
they should be concealed in this life, after death they must
suffer everlasting punishment. This is the doctrine of the
Essenes about the soul—possessing thereby an irresistible
bait for those who have once tasted their philosophy.

"§ 12. There are also some among them who undertake to
foretell future events, having been brought up from their
youth in the study of the sacred Scripture, in divers purifications, and in the sayings of the prophets ; and it is very seldom
that they fail in their predictions.

"§ 13. There is also another order of Essenes who, in their
way of living, customs, and laws exactly agree with the others,
excepting only that they differ from them about marriage.
For they believe that those who do not marry cut off the
principal part of human life—that is, succession—especially
that, if all were of the same opinion, the whole race would
soon be extinguished. They, however, try their spouses for
three years, and after giving evidence, by three natural pur-
gations, that they are fit to bear children, they marry them.
They have no connubial intercourse with them when with
child, to show that they do not marry to gratify lust, but only
to have children. The women, too, have their garments on
when they have baths, just as the men have on their aprons.
Such are the customs of this brotherhood."

The next mention which Josephus makes of them is in his
Antiq. Book xiii. chap. v. § 9, and is as follows :—

"§ 9. At this time [166 B.C.] there were three sects ($\alpha\iota\rho\acute{\epsilon}\sigma\epsilon\iota\varsigma$)

D

among the Jews, differing in their opinion about human affairs. The first was called the sect of the Pharisees, the second the sect of the Sadducees, and the third the sect of the Essenes. The Pharisees affirm that some things only, but not all, are the work of fate (τῆς εἱμαρμένης), and some are in our own power, whether they should take place or whether they should not occur; the sect of the Essenes maintain that fate governs all things,[48] and that nothing can befal man contrary to its determination and will (ψῆφος); whilst the Sadducees reject fate, saying that there is no such thing, and that human events do not proceed from it, and ascribe all to ourselves, so that we ourselves are the cause of our fortunes, and receive what is evil from our own inconsiderateness. However, I have given a more minute description of this in the second book of the Jewish War."

He speaks of them again in Antiq. Book xv. chap. x. § 4, towards the end, and § 5, as follows:—

"§ 4. The Essenes, as we call them, were also exempted from this necessity [of taking an oath of allegiance to Herod]. These men live the same kind of life which among the Greeks has been ordered by Pythagoras.[49] I have discoursed more fully about them elsewhere. The reason, however, why Herod had the Essenes in such honour, and thought more highly of them than of mortal nature, is worthy of record. For this account, too, is not unsuitable for this history, inasmuch as it shows the people's opinion about the Essenes.

"§ 5. There was a certain Essene, named Menahem (Μενάημος

48 It is evident that Josephus, as an orthodox and pious Jew, cannot mean by εἱμαρμένη the *Fatum* of the Stoics, which was above the deities; but intends to convey thereby the idea of *eternal counsels* and *predestination* spoken of in the Bible. Indeed, elsewhere Josephus tells us distinctly that "the doctrine of the Essenes delights to leave all things to God" (*vide infra p.* 52); so that that which is in the one case ascribed to *fate*, is in the other ascribed to *God.*

49 No more regard is to be paid to this remark, that the Essenes are like the Pythagoreans, than to the assertion which Josephus makes afterwards that they are related in their manner of life to the Polistae, (*vide infra p.* 53), as his aim was to shew how much the Jewish sects resembled the Greek systems of philosophy. Comp. p. 41, note 21.

= מנחם) who was celebrated not only for the uprightness of his conduct, but also for the fore-knowledge of the future proceeding from God. When he once saw Herod, as a boy going to school, he addressed him by the name of 'King of the Jews.'[50] Herod thought that he did not know him or that he jested, and reminded him that he was of common origin. But Menahem smiled on him most friendlily, clapped him on the back with his hand, and said—'Thou wilt, nevertheless, be king, and wilt begin thy reign happily, for God has found thee worthy of it. And remember the blows that Menahem has given thee, as being the symbol of the change of thy fortune. For this assurance will be salutary for thee when thou wilt love justice and piety towards God and equity towards thy citizens. However, I know that thou wilt not be such a one, for I can perceive it all. Thou wilt, indeed, excel more than any one in happiness, and obtain an everlasting reputation, but thou wilt forget piety and justice. This will not be concealed from God, for he will visit thee with his wrath for it, towards the end of thy life.' Herod paid very little attention to it at that time, as he had no hope of it. But as he soon afterwards advanced to the dignity of king and was happy, he ordered Menahem to come to him in the height of his dominion, and asked him how long he should reign; but Menahem did not tell him. Seeing that he was silent, he asked again whether he should reign ten years. Whereupon he replied, 'Yes; twenty, nay, thirty years;' but did not determine the exact limit of his reign. Herod, rejoicing on it, gave Menahem his hand and dismissed him, and from that time continued to honour the Essenes. I thought of relating this to the readers (though to some it may seem incredible), and of making

50 The fact that Menahem saw Herod in Jerusalem, and that the Essene Judah, as Josephus tells us elsewhere (comp. *Jewish War*, book i. chap. iii. § 5; *Antiq.* book xiii. chap. xi. § 2), foretold in the temple the death of Antigones, clearly shows that the Essenes did not at first form a separate community, but lived together with the rest of their Jewish brethren.

it known, as it concerns us, because many of the Essenes are highly esteemed for their virtuous conduct and knowledge of Divine things."

Josephus also relates instances in which Essenes foretold future events, in Antiq., book xviii., chap. ii., § 2 ; book xviii., chap. xiii. § 3 ; and Jewish War, book 1, chap. iii., § 5.

The last account which Josephus gives us is to be found in his Antiq., book xviii., chap. i., § 2 and 5.

" § 2. There have been three philosophies among the Jews ever since the ancient time of the fathers (ἐκ τοῦ πάνναρχαίου τῶν πατρίων), that of the Essenes, and that of the Sadducees, and a third which the so-called Pharisees followed. Although I have already spoken of them in the second book of the Jewish War, yet will I mention here also something about them.

" § 5. The doctrine of the Essenes delights in leaving all to God (Θεῷ καταλιπεῖν φιλεῖ τὰ πάντα). They regard the soul as immortal, and say that the attainment to virtue must be fought for with all our might. Although they send consecrated gifts to the Temple, yet they never bring any sacrifice on account of the different rules of purity which they observe ; hence, being excluded from the common sanctuary, they offer sacrifices in themselves (spiritually). Otherwise, they are in their manner of life the best of men, and employ themselves wholly in the labour of agriculture. Their uprightness is to be admired above all others who endeavour to practice virtue ; such uprightness, which is by no means to be found among the Greeks and foreigners, is not of recent date, but has existed among them from times of yore (ἐκ παλαιοῦ), striving most scrupulously not to disturb the community of goods, and that the rich should not enjoy more of the common property than the poor. This is the conduct of this people who are more than four thousand in number. They never marry wives, nor endeavour after the possession of property ;

for they believe that the latter leads to injustice, and the former yields opportunities for domestic discord. Living by themselves they serve each other. They choose good men, who are also priests, to be the stewards of their incomes and the produce of the fields, as well as to procure the corn and food. They do not differ at all in their living, but are more like those whom the Dacae call Polistae."

We notice next the account of Caius Julius Solinus, the author of the Geographical compendium called *Polyhistor*, who flourished about 238 A.D. His accounts, which are to be found in chap. **xxxv.** § 7-10 of his work, are evidently derived from Pliny.

" In the interior of Judea, towards the west, are the Essenes, who differ from the usages of all other nations in their marvellous constitutions, and who, according to my opinion, have been appointed by divine providence for this mode of life. No woman is to be found there; connubial pleasures they have entirely renounced; money they know not, and palm-berries are their food.[51] Not a single birth takes place there, and yet there is no want of population. The place itself is devoted to modesty. Although a very large number of persons run to it from all quarters, yet none is admitted who is not thought to possess purity, fidelity and innocence; for, if one has been guilty of the slightest misdemeanour, though he endeavour to obtain admission by offering never so large a fortune, he is excluded by a divine decree. Thus it is that through an immense space of ages *(per immensum spatium saeculorum)*, incredible to relate,[52] this society is perpetuated though no child is born among them."

51 Pliny, whom Solinus copies, simply says that the Essenes live in the society of palm-trees (*socia palmarum*), to form an antithesis with the appellation *a solitary community* (*sola gens*); and this is perfectly correct. But Solinus' alteration of it into " palm-berries are their food " (*palmis victitant*) is incorrect, inasmuch as they lived from the cultivation of the land, bees, &c.

52 This is simply a reiteration of what Pliny says about the antiquity of the Essenes.

The next account is that of Porphyry, the neo-Platonic philosopher and celebrated antagonist of Christianity, who was born 233 A.D. and died about 306 A.D. His description of the Essenes, which is given in his treatise *On the Abstinence from Animal Food (Lugduni ap. Morillon*, 1620, *p.* 381, *&c.)*, is, as he himself tells us, taken from Josephus. He has, however, made some alterations, as may be seen from the following :

" There were three sorts of philosophers among the Jews, the first were headed by the Pharisees, the second by the Sadducees, and the third, who seemed the most honourable (σεμνοτάτη), by the Essenes. The latter formed such a society as Josephus has described it in different parts of his works, as well as in the second book of the Jewish History, which he composed in seven books, as in the eighteenth book of his Antiquities, which he composed in twenty books, and in the second part to the Greeks.[53]

" The Essenes are Jews by birth, and love one another more than other people. They avoid sensual enjoyments as vices, and regard continence and the power to resist the passions as the first virtue ; they despise marriage and adopt the children of strangers, whilst still young and suitable for instruction, regard them as their own, and train them in their usages. They do not repudiate matrimony and child birth in themselves, but they guard against the sensuality of women. They despise riches, and there is a wonderful community of goods among them. There is no one found among them who occupies a distinguished position through his wealth ; for they have a law that those who enter the society give up their possessions to the brotherhood, so that there is no such thing among them as abjectness of poverty or arrogance of riches ; but the possessions of all put together form a fraternal and common property. If one of them happens to be inadver-

53 This work of Josephus, addressed to the Greeks, is no longer extant.

tently anointed, he immediately washes his whole body; for they regard it as praiseworthy to have a dry skin, and they are always dressed in white. They appoint stewards to manage their common property; and every one, without distinction, is eligible for all the offices.

"They are not confined to one city, but live in different places, and everything they have is at the service of the members who happen to come from another city. Though meeting for the first time they at once salute each other as intimate friends (ἴσασιν ὥσπερ συνήθεις); hence they travel without taking anything with them. They do not change either garments or sandals till they are torn or worn out by age; they neither buy nor sell, but every one gives of that which he has to him that wants it, and receives that which he needs; but even without receiving anything in return they freely communicate to him that wants. Their piety towards God is extraordinary. None of them speak about anything profane before the sun rises; but they offer to it some of the prayers transmitted to them by their forefathers, as if they supplicated it to rise, &c., &c." He repeats almost literally the whole of § 5 of Josephus *On the Jewish War*, book ii. chap. viii., which we have given above, p. 43.

Porphyry omits § 6 of Josephus, but gives, with a few verbal alterations, both the whole of § 7, which describes the admission into the order, and § 8, which describes the punishment. He omits the greater part of § 9, and adds the following statement, which is not to be found in Josephus. "Their food is so poor and scanty that they do not require to ease nature on the Sabbath,[54] which they devote to singing praises to God and to rest." He omits from § 10 the description of the division of the Essenes into four classes, and

---

54 This is simply imaginary; the real reason for it was, that they could not dig on the Sabbath the hole that was requisite for it without, as they thought, violating the sanctity of the day, as to do so was considered a labour.

simply mentions firmness in suffering and death. He also omits from § 11 the whole piece beginning with the words "In harmony with the opinion of the Greeks, &c.;" whilst he not only gives the whole of § 12, but has also the following addition, "With such a manner of life, and with their firm adhesion to truthfulness and piety, there are naturally many among them who can foretel future events, &c.;" and concludes with the words, "This is the nature of the order of the Essenes among the Jews," omitting altogether what Josephus says in § 13 about those Essenes who marry.

Epiphanius, bishop of Constantia and metropolitan of Cyprus, who was born in Bezanduca, a small town of Palestine, in the first part of the fourth century, and died in 403, has also given us some brief notices of the Essenes in his celebrated work *Against the Heretics*. His first notice is to be found in *Adver. Haer.*, lib. i. ord. x. p. 28, ed. Col., 1682, under the title *Against the Essenes and the Samaritans*, and is as follows:

"The Essenes continue in their first position, and have not altered at all. According to them there have been some dissensions among the Gorthenes, in consequence of some difference of opinion which has taken place among them—I mean among the Sebuens, Essenes and Gorthenes. The difference of opinion relates to the following matter. The law of Moses commands the Israelites of all places to come up to Jerusalem to the three festivals, viz., the feasts of the Passover, Pentecost and Tabernacles. As the Jews in Judea and Samaria were largely dispersed, it is supposed that those of them who made their pilgrimage to Jerusalem went through Samaritan cities, and as the Samaritans assemble at the same time to celebrate the festivals, a conflict arose between them."

Epiphanius speaks of them again *(Adv. Haer.*, lib. i. ord. xix. p. 39), and under the title, *Against the Ossenes* (κατά 'Οσσηνῶν), as follows:

"Next follow the Ossenes, who were closely connected with the former sect. They too are Jews, hypocrites in their demeanour, and peculiar people in their conceits.[55] They originated, according to the tradition which I received, in the regions of Nabatea, Itruria, Moabitis and Antilis, ('Aρηλῖτις), in the surrounding neighbourhood of the so-called Dead Sea. . . . The name Ossenes, according to its etymology, signifies *the stout race* (στιβυρὸν γένος). . . . A certain person named Elxai joined them at the time of the Emperor Trajan, after the advent of the Saviour, who was a false prophet. He wrote a so-called prophetical book, which he pretended to be according to divine wisdom. He had a brother named Jeeus, who also misled people in their manner of life, and caused them to err with his doctrine. A Jew by birth, and professing the Jewish doctrines, he did not live according to the Mosaic law, but introduced quite different things, and misled his own sect. . . . He joined the sect of the Ossenes, of which some remnants are still to be found in the same regions of Nabatea and Perea towards Moabitis. These people are now called *Simseans*."[56]

"But hear the Sadducee's nonsense (*comp. ibid., p.* 42) : he rejects the sacrificial and altar services, as repulsive to the Deity, and as things which, according to the meaning of the fathers and the Mosaic law, were never offered to the Lord in a worthy manner. Yet he says that we must pray with our faces to Jerusalem, where the sacrificial altar and the sacrifices have their place. He rejects the eating of animal flesh which is common among the Jews, and other things ; nay, even the sacrificial altar and the sacrificial fire, as being foreign to the

55 This unjust remark about the Essenes, whose exemplary virtues and self-denying life elicited the unqualified admiration of Jews, Greeks, and Romans, is just what might be expected from the bigoted persecutor of heretics, amongst whom he put no less a person than St. Chrysostom.

56 This name may be derived from the Hebrew *Shemesh* (שמש) *sun,* and was most probably given to the Essenes, because of the erroneous notion that they *worshipped the sun.*

Deity. The purifying water, he says, is worthy of God, but the fire is unworthy, because of the declaration of the prophet : ' Children, go ye not there to see the fire of the sacrifices, for ye err ; yea, it is already an error to think such a thing.' ' If you look at the fire very closely,' says he, ' it is still far off. Moreover, go ye not to look at the sacrificial fire, but go ye rather to the doctrine of the water..' There is much more of such idle talk to be found among the Ossenes. "[57]

These are the sources from which writers upon the Essenes have, till within very lately, drawn their information. As to the account of Eusebius (*comp. Hist. Ecclesiast., lib.* ii, *cap.* xvii), to which appeal is often made, it is nothing but a Christianized reproduction of the so-called Philonic description of the Therapeutae. It would therefore be useless to give it. In looking through these accounts, it will be seen that there are only three independent ones among them, namely—Philo's, Josephus's and Pliny's ; as the notice of Solinus is merely a repetition of Pliny, the description of Porphyry is almost a literal reproduction of Josephus ; whilst the distorted scraps of Epiphanius are not only worse than useless, but are unworthy of him, and the account of Eusebius is simply misleading, inasmuch as it is a repetition of an apocryphal story, which has nothing to do with the Essenes.

---

57 The whole of this account is worse than useless, inasmuch as it not only gives us no information whatever about this interesting order, but is positively misleading.

III.

Having given the ancient documents, all that now remains is that I should give a brief sketch of the most important modern literature on the Essenes. In doing this part of my task, as in the former, I shall try as much as it is possible to follow the chronological order.

1513-1577.—Accordingly De Rossi occupies the first position. In his erudite work, called *Meor Enajim*, i.e., *The Light of the Eyes*, which is a Cyclopædia of Biblical literature and criticism, this profound critic gives us a brief notice of this brotherhood, in which he maintains that the Essenes are identical with the Greek sect called *Baithusians* in the Talmud, and *Therapeutae* by Philo. His account is as follows : "It has often appeared to me strange that the Talmud should say nothing whatever about that sect which obtained a good report among the nations. I therefore examined the works of our sages, to ascertain whether I could find in them any distinction made between the Sadducees and the Baithusians. And it appeared to me that though both alike denied the traditional law (התורה שעל פה), yet the Baithusians are no where charged with the sin of denying, like the Sadducees, the immortality of the soul and future judgment. Moreover, I thought of the similarity of the names Baithusians and Essenes (ביתוסים איסיאי), and especially of the manner in which the ancients changed names. Now, owing to the word בית being so frequently found prefixed to names of schools and families, the appellation ביתוסים might easily have originated from a junction of the words בית איסיאי. I also saw the passage in the Talmud, Sabbath, cap. viii, fol. 108, as quoted also in Sopherim, cap. i, which is as follows :—' A Baithusian

asked R. Joshuah whence do we know that phylacteries must
not be written upon the skin of an unclean animal?' To
which he replied—'It is written that the Lord's law may be
in thy mouth, (Exod. xiii, 9) this signifies that phylacteries
must be written upon the skin of an animal which thou canst
take into thy mouth, i.e., eat.' To this he said—'This being
the case, we must also not write the phylacteries upon the skin
of an animal which died;' [for an Israelite is as much forbidden to taste the flesh of it, as to eat an unclean animal.]
Hereupon the Rabbi replied—'I will tell thee a parable, to
make the thing clear. Two men are condemned to death:
the one the king kills, and the other is killed by the exe-
cutioner: now, which of the two dost thou esteem higher?
Surely the one whom the king himself has executed. So the
animal which died, [i.e., which the King of Kings caused
to die] must be preferred to the others.' Whereupon the
Baithusian said—'Accordingly, we ought also to eat it.'
R. Joshuah replied—'The Bible prohibits it (Deut. xiv), and
dost thou want to eat it?' The Baithusian then said—'קלוס
This expression Rashi of blessed memory rightly says is Greek;
i.e. καλόν.' Hence it is to be inferred that the Baithusian
was a Greek; and, indeed, we know from Philo and Josephus
that the Essenes were also Greek Jews, living in Alexandria.
.   .   .   From all these things I easily quieted my mind, and
concluded that the Baithusians are the same as the Essenes.'
Now, from a careful perusal of the account given by Josephus
of the Essenes, it will be seen that he never describes them as
Greek Jews. Besides, this is utterly at variance with ancient
tradition, as the Talmudic authorities most positively declare
that the Baithusians and Sadducees were both alike in doctrine,
that both derived their names from the founder of these sects,
Baithos (ביתוס) and Zadok (צדיק), the disciples of Antigonus
of Soho, and that they gave rise to these sects, through mis-

1 Comp. Meor Enajim, edit. Mantua. 1547, fol. 38 b.

interpreting the following saying of their master [2] which
he had received from Simon the Just : — " Be not like servants
who serve their master for the sake of receiving a reward,
but be ye like servants who serve their master without the
view of receiving a reward," recorded in Aboth. i. 3. Upon
this Aboth d. R. Nathan (cap. v.) remarks, " Antigonus'
two disciples at first continued implicitly to teach this saying
to their disciples, and these again to their disciples. At last,
however, they began to ponder over it, and said—' What did
our fathers mean by this saying ? Is a labourer to labour
all day and not receive his wages in the evening ? Now if
our fathers had believed that there is another world, and a
resurrection of the dead, they would not have spoken thus.'
Hence they dissented from the law, and from them originated
the two sects, the Sadducees and the Baithusians, the Sadducees
from Sadok and the Baithusians from Baithus. They used
gold and silver vessels all the days of their life, not because
they were proud, but because they said that the Pharisees
themselves have a tradition that they afflict themselves
in this world, and have nothing in the world to come." From
this we see that 1. The Baithusians, like the Sadducees,
derived their appellation from the proper name of their
founder, which is *Baithus* ביתוס so that the first part of the
name בית cannot be separated from it. 2. Like the Sadducees,
the Baithusians denied the immortality of the soul and the
existence of angels, whereas the Essenes firmly believed in the
immortality of the soul, and made the angels play a very
important part in their creed. That the Sadducees and the
Baithusians were considered to be identical, or, at all events, to

---

2 אנטיגנוס איש סוכו קבל משמעון הצדיק הוא היה אמר אל תהיו כעבדים המשמשים את
הרב על מנת לקבל פרס אלא היו כעבדים המשמשים את הרב שלא על מנת לקבל פרס וחיו
מורא שמים עליכם כדי שיהיה שכרכם כפול.לעתיד לבא: אנטיגנוס איש סוכו היו לו שני תלמידים
שהיו שונין בדבריו שונין היו לתלמידים ותלמידים להלמידיהם עמדו ודקדקו אחריהן ואמרו מה
ראו אבותינו לומר אמר אפשר שיעשה פועל מלאכה כל היום ולא יטול שכרו ערבית אלא אילו יודעין
אבותינו שיש העולם (אחר) ויש תחיית המתים לא היו אומרים כך עמדו ופירשו מי התורה ונפרצו
מהם שתי פרצות צדוקים וביתוסין צדוקים על שום צדוק ביתוסין על שום ביתוס שהזה משתמש
בכלי זהב וכלי כסף כל ימיו לא היתה דעתו גסה עליו אלא צדוקים אומרים מסורת בית פרושים
שהן מצערין עצמן בעולם הזה ובעולם הבא אין להם כלום:

hold similar doctrines is also evident from the fact that what is in one place of the Talmud ascribed to the former, is in another place ascribed to the latter. Thus, for instance, in Succa 48 *b*. the Sadducees are said to have questioned the necessity of bringing a libation of water on the Feast of Tabernacles; in Tosifta Succa cap. iii. it is ascribed to the Baithusians. In Maccoth, 5, *b*. Chagiga, 16 *b*. it is said that the Sadducees urged that a false witness should only then be executed if the individual whom he had falsely accused had already been executed; in Tosifta Sanhedrin, cap. vi. the same thing is ascribed to the Baithusians. According to Joma, 19 *b*. 53 *a*, the Sadducees would have it that the High Priest should put the incense on the fire outside the Sanctuary on the great Day of Atonement, in Tosifta Joma, cap. 1, and Jerusalem Joma, i. 5, this is also ascribed to the Baithusians. Comp. also 115, b., Megillath Taanith, cap. vi., with Tosifta Jadajim cap ii. And 4. The Baithusians are constantly spoken of as heretics and false witnesses (*comp. Jerusalem Rosh Ha-Shana*, ii, 1 ; *Babl. ibid.* 226), which is utterly at variance with the high character given to the Essenes even by those who belonged to opposite sects.

1587-1643.—Our learned countryman, Dr. Thomas Godwyn occupies the next position. In his interesting and erudite volume, entitled *Moses and Aaron :* which was first published in London 1625, Godwyn devotes *the twelfth chapter of the first book* to the Essenes. The etymology of this name he takes to be the Syriac אסא *to heal, to cure diseases*, and submits that they were called Essenes = *θεραπευται physicians*, because they cultivated the study of medicine. His summary of their doctrines and practices is made from Josephus' description of them as well as from Philo's reputed account of *the Therapeutae* which has nothing to do with the Palestinian Essenes. Godwyn also gives a number of supposed parallels between the doctrines and practices of

Essenism and Pythagorism. He does not attempt to account
for these resemblances, nor does he try to trace the origin
of the brotherhood. He is, however, certain that they
existed in the time of Judas Maccabæus and "continued
until the day of our Saviour and after; for Philo and Josephus
speak of them as living in their time." He assigns the
following reasons for their not being mentioned in the New
Testament. 1. Their being small in number. 2. "They were
peaceable and quiet, not opposing any; and therefore not so
liable to reproof as the Pharisees and Sadducees, who opposed
each other, and both joined against Christ." 3. They were
passed over in silence in the New Testament just "as the
Rechabites in the Old Testament, of whom there is mention
only once and that obliquely, although their order continued about three hundred years, before this testimony was
given of them by the Prophet Jeremiah." And 4. "Though
the name of the *Essenes* be not found in Scripture, yet we
shall find in St. Paul's Epistles many things reproved, which
were taught in the school of the Essenes. Of this nature
was that advice given unto Timothy:—'*Drink no longer
water, but use a little wine.*' (1 Tim. v. 23). Again,
'*Forbidding to marry, and commanding to abstain from
meats is a doctrine of devils*' (1 Tim. iv. 3); but especially *Colossians* ii., in many passages the Apostle seemeth
directly to point at them, 'Let no man condemn you in meat
and drink' (verse 16): 'Let no man bear rule over you, by
humbleness of mind and worshipping of angels' (verse 18)
'Why are ye subject to ordinances (τί δογματίζεσθε verse 20)?'
The Apostle useth the word δόγματα which was applied by the
Essenes to denote their *ordinances aphorisms* or *constitutions*.
In the verse following he gives an instance of some particulars,
'*Touch not, taste not, handle not*' (ver. 21). Now the
junior company of Essenes might not *touch* the seniors.
And in their diet their taste was limited to bread, salt, water

and hyssop. And these ordinances they undertook διὰ πόθον σοφίας saith Philo, *for the love of wisdom ;* but the Apostle concludeth (ver. 23) that these things had only λόγον σοφίας a show of *wisdom.* And whereas Philo termeth the religion of the Essenes by the name of θεράπεια which word signifieth *religious worship ;* the Apostle termeth in the same verse εθιλεθρεκείαν *voluntary religious worship* or *will worship ;* yea, where he termeth their doctrine πάτρων φιλοσοφίας a kind of *philosophy received* from their forefathers by tradition ; St. Paul biddeth them beware of *philosophy* (ver. 8)." I have given this extract in full because succeeding writers have with more or less exactness based their opinion upon it. In animadverting upon it, I need only refer to the former part of this Essay, where it will be seen that some of the things here mentioned, are not peculiar to the Essenes, and others do not belong to them at all, whilst the last quotation from Philo describes the *Therapeutae* and not the Essenes.[3]

1628-1678.—Next in point of time is Theophilus Gale, who gives us a description of the Essenes in his famous work called *The Court of the Gentiles,* part ii. (Oxford, 1671), book ii. § 9, p. 146-156. As might be expected from this learned writer, who wrote this elaborate work to demonstrate that " the original of all human literature, both philology and philosophy, is from the Scriptures and the Jewish Church," he endeavours to prove that Pythagoras took the whole of his philosophic system from the Essenes. " As for the origination of their name," Gale tells us, " they were called חסדים i.e. according to the Greek καθαροὶ and according to our English dialect *pure.* Now the origination or rise of these Essenes I conceive (by the best conjectures I can make from antiquity), to be in or immediately after the Babylonian captivity (though some make them later), and the occasion of their separation

---

3 Comp. Moses and Aaron: Civil and Ecclesiastical Rites used by the Ancient Hebrews, eighth edition (London, 1672), book i, chap. xii, p. 50-59.

and consociation seems this. Many of the carnal Jews defiling themselves either by being too deeply plunged in worldly
affairs, even to the neglect of their religion, or, which was
worse, by sensual compliances with their idolatrous lords,
thereby to secure their carnal interests, these חסרים or Essenes,
to preserve themselves from these common pollutions, separated and retired themselves from the crowd of worldly affairs
into an holy solitude, and private condition of life ; where they
entered into a strict confederation or consociation to lead
together a collegiate devout life."[4] He then gives an epitome
of their doctrines and practices, and finally endeavours to
shews that Pythagoras got his system from them. In doing
this, Gale mixes up the Therapeutae with the Essenes, and
follows largely the description of Godwyn.

1643-1724.—We then come to Dean Prideaux, who has
a lengthy description of the Essenes in *The Old and New
Testaments Connected*, part ii. book v., which first appeared
in London, 1717. The chief value of Prideaux's work on
this subject consists in the fact, that he has given in English
Philo and Josephus on the Essenes, as well as the short
notice from Pliny. In his own remarks, which follow these
extracts, he, in common with his predecessors, mixes up the
Therapeutae with the Essenes, and tries to repel the Romanists
who adopted the assertion of Eusebius *(Hist. Ecclesiast.
lib.* ii. *c.* 17*)*, that these Therapeutae or contemplative Essenes
were Christian monks instituted by St. Mark. He also endeavours to expose the folly of the Deists, who infer, from the
agreement between the Christian religion and the documents
of the Essenes, that Christ and his followers were no other
than a sect branched out from that of the Essenes. Among
the accusations which the Dean brings against the Essenes
for violating the law of God, is the charge that they " absolutely condemned servitude which the holy Scriptures of the

4 The Court of the Gentiles. Pt. ii of "Philosophy," Oxford, 1671, p. 147, &c.

E

New Testament (Philemon 9-21), as well as the Old, allow."[5]
Instead of blaming them for repudiating slavery, we believe
that the civilized world in the present day will be unanimous
in pronouncing it to have been one of the glorious features of
Essenism, anticipating the spirit of Christianity and the philanthropy of the nineteenth century.

1653-1723.—Basnage gives a very lengthy account of the
Essenes in his History of the Jews *lib.* ii. *chaps.* xii. xiii. Those
who are acquainted with the writings of this learned French-
man, know that he could not write on anything without
bringing together a mass of useful information. He, however,
mistook the character of the Essenes, as well as the value of
the documents upon which he relies. Preferring Philo's
account to that of Josephus, though the latter lived amongst
the Essenes, Basnage confounds the brotherhood with the
Therapeutae, and hence asserts that " they borrowed several
superstitions from the Egyptians, among whom they retired."
Through this, he is led to occupy by far the greater part of
his description with the needless discussion of the question
" Whether the Essenes from being Jews were converted to
Christianity by St. Mark, and founded a monastic life."[6]

1692-1762.—Dr. Jennings' chapter on the Essenes is simply
a commentary on Godwyn's account. Jennings disputes some
of the imaginary parallels between Essenism and Pythagorism
exhibited by Godwyn, and inclines to the opinion " that the
Essenes begun a little before the time of the Maccabees, when
the faithful Jews were forced to fly from the cruel persecutions
of their enemies into deserts and caves, and by living in those
retreats, many of them being habituated to retirement, which
thereby became most agreeable to them, they chose to continue it, even when they might have appeared upon the public

5 The Old and New Testaments Connected, seventeenth editions, vol iii.
London, 1815, part ii, book v, p. 406—431.
6 The History of the Jews, from Jesus Christ to the present day. London,
1708, p. 125—137.

stage again, and accordingly formed themselves into recluses."
As to the difficulty to account for " the absolute silence of the
evangelical history concerning the Essenes," Jennings re-
iterates the remarks of Godwyn upon the subject.[7]

In 1821, appeared in Berlin, Bellermann's valuable little
volume on the Essenes and Therapeutae.[8] The author with
characteristic German industry and perseverance, brought
together in this monograph the ancient documents on the
Essenes. His critical acumen, however, is not commensu-
rate to his industry, and while his little volume will deservedly
continue to be a useful manual for the student who wishes to
acquaint himself with what Philo, Pliny, Josephus, Solinus,
Porphyry, Epiphanius and Eusebius said upon this subject,
it is to be questioned whether Bellermann's conclusions will
be shared by many. He is of opinion that " the Essenes and
Baithusians are the same both in name and doctrine," and
that " the Essenes have four other names in history besides
their proper name, viz. :—they are called, 1, *Therapeutae* by
the Greek Alexandrians. 2. *Hiketeans* by Philo, in the
superscription to the Treatise on contemplative life. 3. *Ossenes*
or *Ossens*, by Epiphanius. And 4, *Baithusians* in the Talmud,
and by several Rabbins. As this notion, which has been
advanced by De Rossi three centuries and a half ago, has
already been refuted, it would be needless to repeat the argu-
ments here.

1825.—Neander, whose first instalment of his gigantic
Church History appeared in 1825, now began to grapple with
this mysterious brotherhood. In the introductory chapter of
this history, in which a description is given of the religious
condition of the world at the advent of Christ, he gives a very

7 Jewish Antiquities ; or a Course of Lectures on the two first books of
Godwyn's Moses and Aaron, ninth edition. London, 1837, book i., chap. xii,
p. 281—287.

8 Geschichtliche Nachrichten aus dem Alterthume über Essäer und Therapeuten. Berlin, 1821.

brief but very pregnant sketch of the Essenes. With that deep penetration, which was one of the chief characteristics of this sagacious critic, he repudiates the notion that the Essenes originated under foreign influences, and maintains that "it is a gross error to infer from the resemblance of certain religious phenomena the relationship of which is to be traced to a common inward cause, inherent in the nature of the human mind, that they have an external origin, having been copied from the other." Hence, he submits that Essenism arose out of the deeper religious meaning of the Old Testament, that it afterwards adopted some of the old Oriental, Parsee, and Chaldean notions, and that it had no Alexandrian elements. Neander moreover most justly cautions against the accounts of Philo and Josephus, saying that they clothed the opinions of the Essenes in a garb peculiarly Grecian, which we might rightly consider as not originally belonging to them.[9]

1829.—The difficulty which perplexed Christian writers, arising from the fact that the Essenes are not mentioned in the New Testament, did not affect Jewish writers, although it is true that this name is also not to be found in the ancient Jewish writings. For if it be granted that this appellation is a corruption of an Aramaic word, the Essenes must be looked for in the Talmud and Midrashim, which are chiefly written in Aramaic, under their original designation whatever that might be. The clue to it must, of course, be the identity of the features ascribed to them by Philo and Josephus and those ascribed in the ancient Jewish volumes to any order of Judaism. To this task Rappaport, the corypheus of Jewish critics, betook himself. Knowing that the Essenes were no distinct sect, in the strict sense of the word, but simply an order of Judaism, and that there never was a rupture between them and the rest of the Jewish community, Rappaport most

9 General History of the Christian Religion and Church, English Translation, Clark's Theological Library, vol. i, Edinburgh, 1851, p. 58—66.

justly does not expect that they would be spoken of under a
fixed denominational name. He therefore rejects De Rossi's
notion that the Baithusians, so frequently denounced in the
Talmud and Midrashim, are the Essenes described by Philo
and Josephus, and sought to identify them by their peculiar
practices, expecting to find that they would be spoken of by
different names. He soon found that what Philo and Josephus describe as peculiarities of the Essenes tallies with what
the Mishna, the Talmud, and the Midrashim record of the
Chassidim (חסדים), and that they are most probably the so-
called *old believers* (ותיקין), who are also described in the
Talmud as *the holy community in Jerusalem* (קהלא קדישא
דבירושלים). He rightly recognised in them an intensified form
of Pharisaism, and remarks that what is said in the Mishna
about the moderation observed in eating and drinking, the
great humility, endurance under sufferings, zeal for everything
that is holy, community of goods, &c., refers to this holy community, or the Essenes. He also quotes the following remark
from the Midrash Coheleth, on Eccles. ix, 9, about this holy
community; "Rabi repeated from the traditions of the holy
community (עדה קדושה) ' acquire a trade in connection with
the study of the Scriptures, &c.'—[Query] 'Why are they
called holy community?' [Reply] 'Because they divided the
day into three divisions—devoting one-third to the study of
the Scriptures, another to prayer, and the third to work.
Some say that they devoted the whole of the winter to studying the Scriptures and the summer to work.'" He, too, was
the first who pointed out that the prayer which Josephus tells
us the Essenes offered up at the rising of the sun, is the
national hymn of praise, which still constitutes a part of the
Jewish daily service, and is as follows :—

He in mercy causes His light to shine upon the earth and upon the
inhabitants thereof; and in His goodness unfailingly renews every day
the work of creation. How numerous are Thy works, O Lord! Thou
hast made them all in wisdom; the earth is full of Thy possessions.

O King, Thou only art the exalted one from everlasting, the praised and glorified and extolled since the days of yore! Lord of the universe, in Thy great mercy have mercy upon us! Lord our might, fortress of our strength, shield of our salvation, defend us! O Lord, be Thou praised, Thou great in wisdom, who hast ordained and created the rays of the sun: the Infinitely Good has formed a glorious testimony for His name. He surrounded His majesty with luminaries The chiefs of His heavenly hosts are holy beings; they glorify the Almighty; they continually declare the glory of God and his holiness. Blessed be the Lord our God, for the excellency of the works of Thy hands, and for the shining luminaries which Thou hast. They shall glorify Thee for ever.

God, the Lord of all created things, is praised and blessed in the mouths of all the living. His power and goodness fill the universe; wisdom and intelligence are round about Him. He exalts himself above the angels, and beams in glory upon his chariot-throne. Interceding goodness and rectitude are before His throne, loving-kindness and mercy before his majesty. Benign are the luminaries which our God has created. He has formed them in wisdom, intelligence, and understanding; He has endowed them with power and strength, to bear rule in the midst of the world. Filled with splendour and brightness, their glory illuminates all the world; rejoicing in rising and joyous in setting they perform with awe the will of their Creator. They give praise and glory to His name, joy and song to the memory of His kingdom. He called the sun, and light rose; He saw and shaped the form of the moon. Praise Him all ye heavenly hosts; ascribe glory and majesty to Him ye seraphim, ophanim, and holy angels.

These, as Rappaport rightly remarks, are some of the remains of the ancient prayer used by the Essenes. It will be seen that these hymns of praise contain not only thanksgiving for the renewal of the light, to which Josephus refers, but they also refer to the mysterious cosmogony (מעשה בראשית) and theosophy (מעשה מרכבה), as well as to the angels which played such an important part among this brotherhood.[10]

1835.—The difficulty of reading Rabbinical Hebrew in which Rappaport's profound remarks are written, must have prevented Gfrörer from seeing what this erudite Jewish critic had written on the Essenes; for, although the second edition of vol. i. part 11 *of his Critical History of Primitive Christianity*, containing an account of the Essenes, appeared in 1835, yet he positively states " that the Essenes and the Therapeutae are the same sect and hold the same views" (p.299).

10 Rappaport, in the Hebrew Annual, entitled Bikure Ha-Ittim, vol. x, Vienna, 1829, p. 118 ff.

According to him, the development of Essenism is as follows. In the third century before Christ, the Jews in Alexandria formed societies according to the Pythagorean model, and thus originated the sect called the Therapeutae, from these Egyptian Therapeutae again Essenism developed itself in Palestine about 130 B.C. Hence Essenism is the channel through which the Alexandrian theosophy was first transplanted into Palestinian soil. The reason why the Essenes kept their doctrines secret is that the Palestinian priests were hostile to this foreign importation, and persecuted those who received this contraband. Accordingly, the relationship of Pythagorism, Therapeutism and Essenism, to use Gfrörer's own figure, is that of grandmother, mother and daughter. " So perfect is the agreement between the Therapeutae and the Essenes, that it even extends to their names. For the word 'Εσσαῖνς, according to the most correct etymology, is derived from the Syro-Chaldaic verb אסא which denotes *to cure, to nurse*, and hence is nothing but a literal translation of θεραπευτὴς."[11]

1843.—Similar in spirit is the elaborate article on the Essenes in *Ersch und Gruber's Cyclopœdia*, written by Dähne, who maintains that " Essenism is the produce of the Jewish-Alexandrian philosophy, and that it is only when viewed from this stand-point that the deviations from the rest of their Jewish co-religionists, and their peculiar institutions, doctrines, and precepts appear in the clearest light." It is not surprising that holding such an opinion Dähne should feel perplexed to account for the existence of this thoroughly Jewish-Alexandrian order, as he makes the Essenes to be, in the very heart of Palestine. All that he can say upon this subject is, that they somehow got there in the middle of the second century before Christ. The affiliation of Essenism to the Jewish-

11 Comp. Kritische Geschichte des Urchristenthums. 1 Theil Philo und die jüdish-alexandrianische Theosophie, 11 Abtheilung. Stuttgart, 1835. p. 299–356.

Alexandrian philosophy brings it into most intimate relationship with Therapeutism, and necessarily devolves upon Dähne
to define this family connection which he does in the following
manner.[12] The difference between the Therapeutae and the
Essenes, both of whom are followers of the Jewish-Alexandrian
moral philosphy, is that the former devoted themselves entirely
to a contemplative life, whilst the latter gave themselves more
especially to a practical life. Hence though both rest upon
the same foundation, the Therapeutae gave themselves up
absolutely to the highest aim of man, as they marked it out,
the contemplation of God; whilst the Essenes to some extent
voluntarily lingered in the outer court of the Holy of Holies,
placed themselves intentionally for the good of the brethren
in more frequent contact with the world than the requirements
of nature demanded, thereby generously, but certainly unphilo-
sophically, temporarily retarding their own highest perfection
and happiness." Like De Rossi, Bellermann, Gfrörer and
others, Dähne derives the name from the Chaldee אסא *to heal*,
and says "accordingly the term Essenes denotes *spiritual
physicians*, or men who strive in the highest sense to lead
back the spirit to its natural (i.e. truly divine) character and
activity." [13]

1846.—A new epoch began in the history of the Essenes
with the investigation of Frankel on this subject, which

12 Diese Trennung nun aber unter ben Anhängern der jüdisch-alexandrinischen
Religionsphilosophie selbst in solche, welche sich ausschliesslich dem beschau-
lichen und in Andere, welche sich vorzugsweise dem praktischen Leben widmeten,
ist es eben, welche sich in unserem fraglichen Doppelorden auch äusserlich
repräsentirte, sodass, wenn schon beide ganz auf derselben philosophischen
Unterlage ruhten, die Therapeuten sich möglichst ausschliesslich und unmittelbar
dem höchsten von ihnen angestrebten menschlichen Lebensziele, der Anschauung
Gottes selbst, hingaben, während die Essäer gewissermassen freiwillig in dem
Vorhofe zum Allerheiligsten zögernd, sich absichtlich und zum Besten der Brüder
häufiger in Berührung setzten mit dem Sinnlichen, als es die Naturnothwendig-
keit foderte und so ihre eigene höchste Vollkommenheit und Seligkeit zwar
grossmüthig, aber gewiss auch unphilosophisch genug augenblicklich noch
verkümmerten.

13 Comp. Ersch und Gruber's Allgemeine Encyklopädie, section i. vol. xxxviii.
p. 173-192.

appeared in his *Zeitschrift für die religiözen Interesse des Judenthums*, 1846. Taking up the idea of Rappaport, that the Essenes must be looked for in the body of the Jews and not as a separate sect, Frankel refers to the fact that, whilst the *Assideans = Chassidim* are referred to in 1 Macc. ii. 24; 2 Macc. xiv. 6. &c., the *Perushim = Pharisees* are never mentioned, to show that no such marked and denominational divisions existed at first in the community, and rightly remarks, that it " is only after a longer development that sects appear in their separation, and sharply defined features, when that which originally formed a united whole is now divided and parted into various branches. And even this partition and separation only shew themselves to the analysing mind, and especially when the analysis is conducted after a foreign fashion, as Josephus has done it, who reduced the Jewish sects into Greek schools, and made the Essenes correspond to the Pythagoreans. But in reality even these divisions flow one into another, and do not stand in opposition to one another, but are simply to be distinguished by their different shades of colour, and by the greater stringency or laxity with which the same rules are regarded, so that they do not form separate sects, but some individuals keep to these rules with greater anxiety, whilst others, though considering them as binding, do not regard them as having such a wide application. Now in early times there were only *Essenes = Chassidim* (חסדים), the name of *Perush = Pharisee* (פרוש) was not as yet known; it was only afterwards when in succeeding periods some became more rigid in their manner of life and views of religion, that the name Pharisees (פרושים) appears to denote the less strict Jews, whilst the others were in a special degree denominated by the old, respectable appellation *Chassidim = Essenes* (חסדים)." This, Frankel corroborates by showing most clearly that many of the vital principles which Josephus describes as peculiar to Essenism, are at the very basis of

Pharisaism, and that the Essenes are frequently mentioned in the Mishna, Talmud, and Midrashim by the names חסדים הראשונים *the original Assideans* = *Chassidim*, חברים *the associates*, ותיקין *those who have enfeebled their bodies through much study;* דבירושלים *the retired ones;* צנועין טובלי קהלא קדישא *the holy congregation in Jerusalem;* שחרית *hemerobaptists.* Frankel concluded his essay with the promise to return to this subject on some future occasion.[14]

1847.—Within twelve months of the publication of Frankel's elaborate Essay, an article appeared in the American Quarterly entitled *The Biblical Repository*. As there was not sufficient time for this German production to become known in the New World, Mr. Hall, the writer of the article, could not avail himself of it, and was therefore obliged to derive his information from the writings of Dr. Neander. But though Mr. Hall has thrown no light on the Essenes, yet his reflections upon their moral character and their connection with Christianity are so just, sensible and candid, that we subjoin them to show that good Christians may honestly acknowledge the good in Essenism without detracting from Christianity.

" Let us give the Essene credit for all that he was as a worshipper of the true God, and as a man striving after moral purity in a corrupt age. The Gospel that breathed new life into the higher nature of man, can afford to allow all his virtues. We know that the Spirit of Christ opens the eye to the excellencies of others. Truth rejoices in truth, and as all truth is from the same source, the lustre of one development can never be increased by hiding the glory of another. We would not enhance the necessity of our Lord's appearance by depreciating the moral condition of mankind at that period. Those ascetic Jews deserve well of mankind for the light they gave out in a dark age. We admire the humanity and justice of their principles; their disapproval of war and slavery in the midst of a world lying in wickedness, and the noble example of industry, frugality and moderation in the things of this life they set before all. We honour their honest endeavours to combine the *vita contemplativa* and the *vita activa*,—to escape the bondage of the senses, to maintain the supremacy of the spirit, and to unite themselves with the Highest. But in all these respects, they are only the true children of monotheism, the legitimate offspring of the Jewish theocracy. They could have sprung up nowhere else. In the phenomenon of the Essenes let us

14 Comp. Frankel, Zeitschrift für die religiösen Interessen des Judenthums, vol. iii. Berlin, 1846, p. 441-461.

therefore adore the provident wisdom of Jehovah, and recognize the secret working of his love in carrying forward the great, eternal economy of salvation. They exerted an influence on their age which helped to pave the way for the Christ. Conscience spoke, and was spoken to, through them; and the dying sense of virtue was kept alive. Thus were they stars which emitted an humble though useful light before, but grew pale and became invisible after, the coming of the Sun of Righteousness." [15]

1852.—Though Ewald published the second edition of the fourth volume of his Jewish History in 1852, when Frankel's Essay had been six years before the literary world, yet he manifests total ignorance of it in his account of the Essenes, contained in this volume. Still, this profound and merciless critic, without having access to the Jewish information gathered from the Talmud and Midrashim, saw that Essenism was no Greek plant transplanted into Palestine, but like Pharisaism grew out 'of the Chassidim. He remarks that "people, who left the great community in order to lead a specially holy life, with the permission and under the direction of the law, were to be found in Israel from the remotest times, yet in its first form there were only the Nazarites, of whom each one lived for himself; and in the second, the Rechabites combined themselves already into a larger union ; but now the whole conscience of the people itself, as it were, departed into solitude with numerous Essenes. For it cannot be denied that they, proceeding from the Chassidim, represent the direct and legitimate development of Judaism in the form which became the ruling one since Ezra." "Their new features and endeavours merely consisted in their intensely earnest and rigorous application of the demands of the law, as understood and interpreted since Ezra. Finding that the rigorous and logical application of these laws was impossible in the great community, especially in that community as regulated by the Pharisees, they preferred to congregate and

15 Comp. The Biblical Repository and Classical Review. New York, 1847, p. 162–173.

live in solitude." [16]   Very unfortunate is Ewald's derivation of Essene from the Rabbinic חין *servant* (of God), and the assertion that this name was given to them because it was their only desire to be θεραπευταὶ θεοῦ.

1853.—Nearly seven years had now elapsed since Frankel published his masterly Essay on the Essenes, and promised to return to this subject at some future time.   True to his promise, he now gave another elaborate treatise, in which he substantiated, by numerous quotations from the Talmud, his former conclusions, that the Essenes are the offspring of Judaism, that they are nothing but stationary, or more correctly speaking consequential Chassidim, that they were therefore not so far distant from the Pharisees as to be regarded as a separate sect, but, on the contrary, that they formed a branch of Pharisaism.[17]

1856.—So convincing was Frankel's Treatise, that Graetz, who published the third volume of his masterly History of the Jews in 1856, in which he gives an elaborate account of this brotherhood, remarks :[18] " I completely accept these results about this sect being based upon critical investigation, and shall only add a few supplementary points by way of illustration." [19]   The additions consist of a very able analysis of Philo's reputed Treatise entitled *De Vita Contemplativa*, showing that it is spurious, and of an attempt to show that the Essenes were *perpetual Nazarites* (נזירי עולם).   His remarks are as follow—" There were great masses of Nazarites in the

16 Geschichte des Volkes Israel, Vierter Band.   Göttingen, 1852, p. 419–428.

17 Comp. Monatschrift für Geschichte und Wissenschaft des Judenthums, Zweiter Jahrgang.   Leipzig, 1853, p. 30–40; 61–73.

18 Ich nehme diese auf kritischer Forschung, beruhenden Resultate über diese Secte vollständig an und werde nur noch einige Pünkte nachträglich beleuchten.

19 Die Eigenthümlichkeiten der Essäer lassen sich nicht genügend aus dem Wesen der im Talmud vorkommenden חסידים oder חסידים הראשנים und der in der Makkabäerzeit auftretenden „ Assidäer" erklären ; man muss auch auf das nasir-äische Wesen Rücksicht nehmen.   Nasiräer gab es in der nachexilischen Zeit eine grosse Menge (*Tosifta Nasir c.* iv.   *Babli Berachot* 48 *a.* 1 *Makkub.* ii, 49. *Jos. Alterth.* xviii, 6, 1).   Aber sie trugen zugleich einen andern Charakter, als

post-exile period (*Tosifta Nasir, c.* iv.; *Babbi Berachoth*, 48 *a*; 1 *Macc.* ii. 49; *Joseph. Antiq.* xviii. vi.), but they were of a different character to those of the Biblical period; they were *Nazarites for the whole life* (*Nasir* 4 *a*.) The Mishna presupposed their existence; the magical in Nazaritism, which was connected with the growing of the hair in the Nazarites of the Bible, gradually recedes into the back ground or loses its significance altogether; whereas the Levitical, the guarding against defilement, appears more and more in the foreground among the life-long Nazarites. The Essenes then were such Nazarites as represented in private life the highest priestly consecration. The connection between the Nazarites and Essenes has already been indicated in obscure passages in the Talmud, that one consecrated himself to be a perpetual Nazarite if he simply wished to be a Nazarite in order that he

die der biblischen Zeit: sie waren Nasiräer fürs ganze Lebus נזיר עולם (*Nasir* 4 *a*). Die Mischna setzt das Vorhandensein solcher ohne Weiteres voraus, und das Magische an dem Nasiräerthum, das sich bei den biblischen Nasiräern an den Haarwuchs knüpfte, tritt immer mehr zurück, oder hat vielmehr gar keine Bedeutung mehr. נזיר עולם הכביד שערו שיקל בשער (das.). Hingegen tritt bei den lebenslänglichen Nasiräern das Levitische, die Hut vor Verunreinigung, immer mehr in den Vordergrund (das.) Die Essäer werden also solche Nasiräer gewesen sein, welche in ihrem Privatleben die höchste priesterilische Weihe darstellen wollten. Den Zusammenhang zwischen Nasiräern und Essäern deutet schon eine dunkle talmudische Stelle an, dass Jemand sich dadurch schon dem vollständigen Nasireat weiht, wenn er auch nur insofern Nasiräer sein will, um die Geheimnisse entehrender Familienverhältnisse bewahren zu können: הריני נזיר אם לא אגלה משמחות הרי וו נזיר ולא יגלה משמחות (*Tosifta Nasir c.* 1 *b Kiduschim* 71 *a*). Die Erklärung dieser Stelle durch den Essenismus hat schon Edeles (מוהרש"א) in seinem Agadacommentar z. St. geahnt. Diesen Zusammenhang zwischen Nasiräerthum und Essenismus haben Epiphanius und die arabischen Schriftsteller Makrisi und Abulfarag' geahnt; wenn auch Epiphanius die Ναζαραῖοι von den 'Οσσηνοί unterscheidet, die er von den Erstern berichtet, doch ganz essäisch. Ebenso hat Makrisi die Essäer in drei Secten zerspalten, in die Täufer (מנסדין==ἡμεροβαπτισταί), die Essäer (אסאיין) und in die Nasiräer (מחזסון) (in *de Sacy Chrestomathie Arabe* Ausgabe von 1806, arabischer Theil 172 und *tome* ii, 218). Das arabische Makkabäerbuch bezeichnet die Essäer durch Chassidäer (c. xxv); in Josippon fehlen an der Stelle, wo er von den drei Secten spricht, gerade die Essäer (iv, 6, Breithaupt) Die Identität von Nasiräern, Essäern und Assidäern wird also von vielen Seiten bestätigt. Auch aus Josephus' Angabe, die Essäer hätten eigne Bücher gehabt (jüd. Kr. ii, 8, 7), lässt sich ihre Identität mit den Assidäern erweisen. Im Talmud (Jeruschalmi Barachot, Ende) wird aus einem Buche der Chassidäer der Satz mitgetheilt: „Verlässt du sie einen Tag, so verlässt sie dich zwei Tage": כתוב בספר חסידים אם תעובה אם תעובה יום יומים תעובך

might be able to preserve the secrets of disgraceful family circumstances. (*Tosifta Nasir, b.* i. 6 ; *Kidushim* 71 *a.*)[20]

1857.—The learned historian Jost, who published the first volume of his History of Judaism in 1857, was also perfectly convinced by the results of Frankel's researches, and made them the basis of his excellent description of the Essenes, in which he maintains that they grew out of Pharisaism or from the ancient *Chassidim.* "The Essenes," he submits, "are exactly the same that the other Rabbis wished to be who endeavoured to practise the Levitical law of purity, as leading to higher consecration. They have neither another creed nor another law, but simply institutions peculiar to this brotherhood, and endeavour to reach the highest consecration by their manner of life, in defining the different stages, according to preliminary exercises and certain years of preparation. Their views and tenets are therefore also to be found in the utterances of the learned and the Rabbis who did not enter their order, so that they did not look upon the Essenes as opponents or apostates, but, on the contrary, as holding the same opinions with increased claims and some fewer enjoyments, whom many out of their own midst joined, and who were called *Chassidim* or *Zenuim.*"[21]

1857.—The comparatively few and unessential deviations from Judaism to be found in Essenism were, however, more than Herzfeld could tolerate, without characterising the innovators as heretics and smugglers of contraband opinions. Dissatisfied with the modern researches of Frankel and Graetz on this subject, this learned historian, and chief Rabbi of Brunswick, returned to the old notion of De Rossi, that the Essenes of Josephus and Philo are identical with the Baithusians mentioned in the Talmud. Still he thinks that De Rossi's

---

20 Geschichte der Juden, vol. iv. Leipzig, 1856, p. 96–106 ; 518–528.

21 Geschichte des Judenthums und seiner Secten, vol. 1. Leipzig, 1857, p. 207–215.

opinion "must be better proved than he had done it," and
therefore remarks—" first of all, seeing that the prefixed בית
denotes school or sect in the appellations Beth-Shammai,
Beth-Hillel ; that בית הכותים in Tosifta Helem ii. b, and
בי כותאי in Chullin 6 a, denotes *the sect* or *the land* of
Cuttim ; and then that בית סין stands twice Tosifta Succa,
cap. iii., and Tosifta Menachoth cap. x. for Baithusians, can
it mean anything else than *house* or *sect of Essenes* ?   When
אסי *physician* became the name of a sect, an Essene could
not so well be called אסי without ambiguity ; he was therefore
described as one of בית אסי." [22]   Thus much for the origin of
the name, and now let us hear Dr. Herzfeld's theory about the
brotherhood itself.   It is simply this[23]—" A Jew, who became
acquainted with the allegorical exegesis prevalent among the
Alexandrian Jews, and with its mother the Greek wisdom, but
who, like Pythagoras, Plato and Herodotus, had also found

22 Die Essäer waren die Baitusim, wie schon R. Asarja de' Rossi vermuthet
hat ; es muss dies nur besser begründet werden, als von ihm geschehen ist.   Ich
bemerke zu dem Ende erstens, dass wie das vorgesetzte בית auch in den Benen-
nungen Bet-Schammaj, Bet-Hillel Schule oder Fraction bedeutet, so *Tosifta
Kelim* ii, 6 בית הכותים, *Chulin* 6, *a* בי כותאי für die Sekte oder das Land der
Cutim vorkommt ; sodann dass *Tosifta Succa*, K. iii zweimal und *Tosifta Mena-
chot* K. x. für Baitusim בית סין stehet : kann dies wohl etwas Anderes als Haus,
Sekte der Essener bedeuten ?   Als אסי (Arzt) Sektenname wurde, konnte man
den Essäer nicht gut mehr schlechthin אסי nennen, ohne undeutlich zu werden,
man umschrieb ihn daher wohl als Einen vom בית אסי, bildete danach auch
mit Zugrundelegung der Form Essener, das nachgewiesene בית סין, und zog
dann Jenes zusammen, um den einzelnen Essäer zu bezeichnen, gab aber
dieser Form den u-Laut, entweder nachdem man das syrische Wort אסי zuweilen
nach syrischer Weise *osseh*, also dunkel ausgesprochen hatte, woher die Aussprache
Ossener bei Epiphanius herrühren mag, oder was mir noch wahrscheinlicher ist,
indem man dem Worte Peruschim conform Zedukim und Baitusim bildete.

23 Nach allem diesen scheint es, dass ein Jude, welcher mit der unter den
alexandrinischen Juden aufblühenden allegorischen Exegese und mit deren
Erzeugerin, der griechischen Weisheit, bekannt geworden war, daneben aber
auch Gelegenheit gefunden hatte, von ägyptischen Priestern Manches zu lernen,
wie Pythagoras selbst, Platon und Herodot, den Plan gefasst und ausgeführt
habe, eklektisch hieraus und aus dem Judenthume ein speculatives und asketi-
sches System sowie nach demselben aus judäischen Asketen eine Sekte zu
bilden.   Dass es an Solchen nicht gefehlt habe, verbürgt das Vorkommen von
Nasiräern, z. B. nach *Tosifta Nasir* K. iv unter Schimon dem Gerechten, ferner
1 Macc. iii, 49, und von ihrer 800 auf einmal unter Schimon ben Schatach nach
Nasir jer. v, 3.   Dass er aber nicht mit jüdischen Asketen in Aegypten diesen
Versuch machte, geschah vielleicht, weil es damals dort noch an solchen Asketen
fehlte, oder weil er selbst aus Judäa gebürtig sein mochte.

an opportunity to learn some things from Egyptian priests, conceived and carried out the plan, eclectically to form from it and from Judaism a speculative and ascetic system, as well as to organise, according to its model, a sect from the Jewish ascetics." [24] This Alexandrianized Palestinian Jew founded the order of the Essenes in Palestine about 230 B.C.

1857.—Another effort was made in this year to explain the origin of this mysterious brotherhood. Professor Hilgenfeld of Jena, who maintains their genuine Jewish origin, starts the notion that the Essenes belonged to the Apocalytical school, and that they must be regarded as the successors of the ancient prophets, and as constituting the prophetic school. It is only when we view them from this stand point that their precepts and practices can be understood, and that the high antiquity ascribed to them by Josephus (Antiq. xviii. 1, 2) and Pliny (Hist. Nat. v. 17), can be comprehended. This he moreover assures us gives the clue to the explanation of their name. The Hebrew prophets were also called חוים *seers*, which, being in the Aramaic pronunciation חוין, easily gave rise through Greek change of vowels to the name 'Εσσαῖον, 'Εσσηνοί. Hilgenfeld manifests an almost inexcusable ignorance of the labours of Frankel and Graetz on the Essenes.[25]

1860.—A necessarily brief but interesting article on the Essenes, written by the able Mr. Westcott, appeared in Smith's Dictionary of the Bible. The writer wisely availed himself of the labours of Frankel and Jost, and properly traced the origin of the brotherhood to the Chassidim. His fear, however, lest any shining virtues in the Essenes might be thought by some to pale some of the brightness of the Sun of Righteousness, prevented him from appreciating the true

24 Geschichte des Volkes Israel von Vollendung des Zweiten Tempels bis zur Einsetzung des Meckabäers Schimon zum hohen Priester und Fürsten, Zweiter Band. Nordhausen, 1857, p. 368–377 ; 387–409.

25 Die jüdische Apokalyptik in ihrer geschichtlichen Entwickelung. Jena, 1857, p. 245–278.

character of this order, as well as from seeing that they paved the way to Christianity.

1863.—Graetz again, in the second edition of the third volume of his History of the Jews, in which he has an additional chapter on the Rise and Progress of Christianity, goes to the other extreme, and maintains that Jesus simply appropriated to himself the essential features of Essenism," [16] and that primitive Christianity was nothing but an offshoot from Essenism.

1862.—Of the article on the Essenes in Dr. Alexander's valuable edition of Kitto's Cyclopædia of Biblical Literature, being written by me, I can do no more than say that it embodies the substance of this Essay.

1863.—The description of the Essenes in the new edition of Dean Milman's History of the Jews, gives a very imperfect idea both of the development and morality of this brotherhood.[17] The learned Dean seems to be wholly unacquainted with the researches of Frankel and Graetz on this subject. He, however, rightly rejects the notion that Essenism had its origin in Pythagorism.

1847.—After the above was printed, I found a notice of the Essenes in Hirschfeld's work on the *Hagadic Exegesis*, in which he submits that the name Essene may be derived from the Greek ἠϑος *manners, morality, virtue*, that though the Essenes had several things in common with the Therapeutae, yet there was a great difference between the two sects, and that the former rested more on the Bible and on Judaism. Still he affirms that " some Neo-Platonic, Pythagorean and Persian ideas found their way among the Essenes,

16 Geschichte der Juden, Dritter Band Zweite Auflage. Leipzig, 1863, p. 216–252.

17 The History of the Jews from the earliest period down to modern times. London, 1863, vol. ii. p. 110–115.

F

and brought with them some practices and institutions which this brotherhood mixed up with the Jewish views of religion, and amongst which are to be classed their extension of the laws of purification, &c." Hirschfeld, moreover, maintains that, "like the Alexandrians, but only from a different standpoint, the Essenes aimed to reconcile religion with science." As this opinion has already been discussed in this Essay, it is needless to repeat the objections against it.[18]

18 "Sie lieferte zwar nicht wissenschaftliche Resultate, aber ihr Leben deutet sattsam darauf hin, dass ihre Bestrebungen darauf gerichtet waren, wie in Alexandrien, nur von einem andern Standpunct aus, die Religion und die Wissenschaft zu versöhnen." Der Geist der ersten Schriftauslegungen order: Die hagadische Exegese. Berlin, 1847, p. 114, &c.

New Orleans Scottish Rite College

http://www.youtube.com/c/NewOrleansScottishRiteCollege

Clear, Easy to Watch
Scottish Rite and Craft Lodge
Video Education

Metaphysical/Rosicrucian Books from Cornerstone

The History of Magic
by Eliphas Levi
Translated by Arthur Edward Waite
6x9 Softcover 594 pages
ISBN 1613421559

An Esoteric Reading of Biblical Symbolism
by Harriet Tuttle Bartlett
6x9 Softcover 232 pages
ISBN 1613420803

The Turba Philosophorum
by Arthur Edward Waite
6x9 Softcover 226 pages
ISBN: 1613422091

The Initiates of the Flame
by Manly P. Hall
6x9 Softcover 96 pages
ISBN 1613421990

The Symbolism of Colour
by Ellen Conroy
6x9 Softcover 80 pages
ISBN 1613420838

Isis Unveiled
A Master-Key to the Mysteries of Ancient and Modern Science and Theology
by H.P. Blavatsky
6x9 Softcover 2 volume set 1,374 pages
ISBN 978-1-61342-298-4

Metaphysical/Rosicrucian Books from Cornerstone

Simplified Scientific Astrology
by Max Heindel
6x9 Softcover 204 pages
ISBN 1613420749

Zanoni - A Rosicrucian Tale
by Edward Bulwer Lytton
6x9 Softcover 306 pages
ISBN 161342051X

Initiation and its Results
by Rudolf Steiner
6x9 Softcover 134 pages
ISBN 1613420927

The Minor Prophets
by F. W. Farrar
6x9 Softcover 252 pages
ISBN 1613421079

Esoteric Teachings: the Writings of Annie Besant
by Annie Besant
Edited by Michael R Poll
6x9 Softcover 252 pages
ISBN 1-452854-20-3

Angelic Wisdom:
Concerning the Divine Love and the Divine Wisdom
by Emanuel Swendenborg
6x9 Softcover 388 pages
ISBN 1613420889

Metaphysical/Rosicrucian Books from Cornerstone

Esoteric Christianity
by Annie Besant
6x9 Softcover 170 pages
ISBN 1-934935-47-6

Raja Yoga
by Yogi Ramacharaka
6x9 Softcover 190 pages
ISBN: 161342065X

The Divine Origin of the Craft of the Herbalist
by E. A. Wallis Budge
6x9 Softcover 116 pages
ISBN 1613421222

The Masters and The Path
by C.W. Leadbeater
Foreword by Annie Besant
6x9 Softcover 252 pages
ISBN: 1-887560-80-7

The Rosetta Stone
by E. A. Wallis Budge
6x9 Softcover 210 pages
ISBN 1613421540

The Diaries of Leonardo Da Vinci
Jean Paul Richter, Translator
Michael R. Poll, Editor
Large Format, 7 x 10 Softcover 610 pages
ISBN: 1-887560-84-X

Metaphysical/Rosicrucian Books from Cornerstone

Alchemy: Ancient and Modern
by H. Stanley Redgrove
6x9 Softcover 160 pages
ISBN 1613420846

An Introduction to the Study of the Tarot
by Paul Foster Case
6x9 Softcover 102 pages
ISBN: 1-934935-19-0

Occult Science in Medicine
by Franz Hartmann
6 x 9 Softcover 110 pages
ISBN 1613421133

In the Pronaos of the Temple of Wisdom
by Franz Hartmann
6x9 Softcover 138 pages
ISBN 1-453766-86-3

Numbers: Their Occult Power And Mystic Virtues
by W. Wynn Westcott
6x9 Softcover 140 pages
ISBN 1-934935-55-5

Francis Bacon and His Secret Society
by Constance M. Pott
6x9 Softcover 426 pages
ISBN: 1-934935-28-X

Ancient and Modern Initiation
by Max Heindel
6x9 Softcover 96 pages
ISBN: 1-887560-18-1

Cornerstone Book Publishers
www.cornerstonepublishers.com

Metaphysical/Rosicrucian Books from Cornerstone

The Gates of Knowledge
by Rudolf Steiner
6x9 Softcover 192 pages
ISBN: 1613420935

History of the Secret Societies of the Army
by Charles Nodier
6x9 Softcover 260 pages
ISBN: 1-934935-24-7

The Magical Writings of Thomas Vaughan
by Arthur Edward Waite
Softcover 196 pages
ISBN 1613420773

The Interpretation of Dreams
by Sigmund Freud
6x9 Softcover 524 pages
ISBN 1613420811

Control of Mind and Body
by Frances Gulick Jewett
6x9 Softcover 280 pages
ISBN 161342079X

The Hand-Book of Astrology
by Zadkiel Tao-Sze
6x9 Softcover 126 pages
ISBN 1613420897

Letters on Occult Meditation
by Alice A. Bailey
6x9 Softcover 372 pages
ISBN 1613420978

Cornerstone Book Publishers
www.cornerstonepublishers.com

Metaphysical/Rosicrucian Books from Cornerstone

The Ancient Wisdom
by Annie Besant
6x9 Softcover 178 pages
ISBN: 1-934935-08-5

A Journey into Theosophy
by C.W. Leadbetter
6x9 Softcover 218 pages
ISBN: 1-887560-93-9

The Trial of Jeanne D'Arc
trans. by W.P. Barrett
Large Format, 8.5 x 11 Softcover 250 pages
ISBN: 1-934935-05-0

The Stone of the Philosophers
An Alchemical Handbook
Edited by Michael R. Poll
6x9 Softcover 368 pages
ISBN: 1-887560-85-8

Invisible Helpers
by C. W. Leadbeater
6x9 Softcover 106 pages
ISBN 1-453656-79-0

Wisdom of the Ages:
Revelations from Zertoulem, the Prophet of Tlaskanata
by Rev. George A. Fuller M.D.
6x9 Softcover 118 pages
ISBN 1613420676

Cornerstone Book Publishers
www.cornerstonepublishers.com

Metaphysical/Rosicrucian Books from Cornerstone

The Hermetic Museum
by A.E. Waite
Large Format, 8 x 10 Softcover 421 pages
ISBN 1-887560-98-X

Abraham Lincoln: The Practical Mystic
by Francis Grierson
6x9 Softcover 108 pages
ISBN 1613421117

The Quest of the Historical Jesus
by Albert Schweitzer
6x9 Softcover 428 pages
ISBN 1613422075

Initiation, Human and Solar
by Alice A. Bailey
6x9 Softcover 168 pages
ISBN 1613420714

The Canon
An Exposition of the Pagan Mystery Perpetuated
in the Cabala as the Rule of All Arts
by William Stirling
6x9 Softcover 428 pages
ISBN 1613420854

Treasured Hermetic and Alchemical Writings of Paracelsus
Trans. by A. E. Waite
6x9 Softcover 122 pages
ISBN 1-934935-43-3

Metaphysical/Rosicrucian Books from Cornerstone

The Rosicrucians: Their Teachings
by R. Swinburne Clymer
6x9 Softcover 218 pages
ISBN 1613422024

Egyptian Magic
by E. A. Wallis Budge
6x9 Softcover 256 pages
ISBN 1613421249

The Occult Life of Jesus of Nazareth
by Alexander Smyth
6x9 Softcover 326 pages
ISBN 1613420986

Collectanea Hermetica
Edited by W. Wynn Westcott
Foreword by Clayton J. Borne, III
Large Format 8.5x11 Softcover 722 pages
ISBN 1-61342-018-8

In the Pronaos of the Temple of Wisdom
by Franz Hartmann
6x9 Softcover 138 pages
Retail Price: $16.95
ISBN 1-453766-86-3

The Masters and The Path
by C.W. Leadbeater
Foreword by Annie Besant
6x9 Softcover 252 pages
ISBN 1613421443

Cornerstone Book Publishers
www.cornerstonepublishers.com

Made in United States
North Haven, CT
06 May 2024

52193877R10057